The Art of Connecting

Other Books by Kelly Lowe

An Astrologer's Journey
My Life With The Stars

The Sun Always Rises
How To Thrive In Times of Loss

The Art of Connecting

Feeding Your Soul

Kelly Lowe

CHB Media
Publisher

Copyright 2020 © Kelly Lowe

All Rights Reserved
including the right of reproduction,
copying, or storage in any form
or means, including electronic,
in whole or part,
without prior written
permission of the author.

ISBN: 9781656146182

Front and Back Cover Photos by Kelly Lowe

CHB Media, Publisher

(386) 690-9295
chbmedia@gmail.com

Contents

Foreword: A Deep Knowledge 7
Introduction/Acknowledgements: A Reason For Being ... 8
More About Kelly Lowe 10
Preface: Of Joy And Loneliness 11

SECTION ONE 13
From The Heart
You Can't Sing The Blues Unless You've Had Them

SECTION TWO 19
Connection And Loneliness In The Popular Culture
Jimmy Buffet 20
Sex And The City 24
Dolly Parton 26
Patrick Swayze 28
Internet Dating 29
Hurricanes And Natural Disasters 31

SECTION THREE 33
Natural Gifts To Feed the Soul
Yoga And Connection 34
Reiki 36
Biofield Tuning 38
Healthy Eating for Mental Health 41
Exercise: The Multi-Purpose Therapy 43
Essential Oils To Help With Depression 49
Qigong As A Spiritual Practice 52

SECTION FOUR 55
What Healers Say About Loneliness,
Depression And The Importance Of Connection
Superficial Connections Just Don't Work 56
A Correlation With Internet Access 58
Depression In Our Youth 66
The Strategies Of Shy People 71

SECTION FIVE........73
**The Many Paths To Connection:
As Varied As Life's Adventures**

A Personal Journey After My Husband's Death 74
Travel As An Antidote 82
Life Is Always Evolving...........................88
Connection Begins With The Self 95
A Lunar Tool To Connect With Emotions............108
Inspired By Elizabeth Gilbert 119
Connecting With Your Sun Sign....................133
Celine Dion Says Learn From It, Use It...........141
Of Friends And Lovers 151
New Beginnings After Divorce 156
Our Thoughts Create Who We Are...................163
Volunteering: A Proven Path To Connection 167
When The Unthinkable Happens.....................174
Other Voices, Other Stories......................180
Reinvention Goes More Than Skin Deep.............183
Restored By Faith 185
A Conscious Decision To Move Forward 190
Two Years Later, Life Continues..................193

SECTION SIX 200
More Wisdom To Feed The Soul

Depression Or Loneliness?........................201
Stop Trying To Be Happy 205

Foreword

I have been working with Kelly Lowe for close to 10 years now as her editor and publisher. When I began work on her first book, *An Astrologer's Journey: My Life with the Stars*, I made a surprising discovery about what it means to be an astrological counselor. To that point all I knew about astrology was the shorthand horoscope suggestions for the sun signs published in daily newspapers. What I learned from Kelly was a simple truth: people don't come to her because they are interested in astrology, they come because they have real concerns: relationships, finances, or simply how to make sense out of life. I saw right away that Kelly is adept at combining what the astrological charts say with her deep knowledge of the human condition in order to offer guidance to her clients. I also learned why she is so skilled: she herself has traveled the seeker's path to greater wisdom about the essence of life. What she discovered for herself is shared with readers of her books and with those who come to her for counseling.

Kelly continued her journey in her second book, *The Sun Always Rises*, in which she taught a path to personal recovery and prosperity following times of loss. This book, *The Art of Connecting*, guides the reader onward to the next step—feeding your soul as you move toward a full and abundant life.

— Gary Broughman
Publisher, CHB Media

Introduction and Acknowledgements
A Reason for Being ...

Every book should have a reason for being, a purpose, an essential truth it endeavors to convey. Here is mine, as concisely as I can state it without oversimplifying:

Being alone and being lonely are not the same thing. To be alone simply says we are not in the company of other people; to be lonely suggests we are missing something—a connection to others or to yourself. It is said that we come into this world alone and eventually leave it the same way, and yet we know that we are social creatures who hunger throughout life for the joy which comes from connecting to others. In *The Art of Connecting ... Feeding Your Soul* I hold out two hopes—the first is to embrace the gift of being comfortable—at one—with yourself, and the second is to experience the joy found only in connecting with others—in whatever way that takes form. In truth these things happen together, or at least in no specified order, but usually when one hope is realized the other appears as well. If there is a true path to contentment in life, I believe this is it.

Part of my goal here is to visit loneliness and connection as they happen in the real world with real people, not to reveal some magic panacea of words. In the end it's up to each of us to find our best way through. So, what I offer in these pages is guidance, possibilities, the experiences of others, and the thoughts of healing practitioners. May they help guide you on your journey to the joy that you are meant to know.

A special thank you to those who shared their wisdom and understanding, to those who shared their stories and have allowed me to share them with my readers, and to those who have inspired me and encouraged me to "feed my soul" by writing this book.

In addition to my family and friends who have been so very supportive of me, I want to extend a special thank you to the professional healers and counselors who have shared their knowledge and experience with me. Without there help and support this book would not have been possible: Katherine M. Billiot, PsyD; Dr. Sandra Brooks; Marcy Chereskin, RN, MSN; Wendy Crain, LMFT; Krista Oakes, Yoga Instructor, E-RYT; Judy W. Stamper, LMHC; and Valerie G. Watt, PhyD, LCSW.

More About Kelly Lowe

Kelly Lowe is an astrological counselor, teacher, and author. She has been a professional astrological counselor for more than 30 years, helping her clients to better understand themselves, and to cope with challenging cycles in their lives.

Kelly believes that her faith in God and understanding of astrology have been the keys to recovering from her own losses and challenging cycles, including an early divorce, and the death of two wonderful husbands. Her life and journey are a testament to recovery and prosperity. Her joy is helping others do the same.

Kelly has appeared on national TV, been a regular guest on several radio shows, and publishes a monthly astrology newsletter. She has taught astrology at Seminole State College and Daytona State College, and gives frequent astrological lectures throughout the country.

Her first book, An *Astrologer's Journey*, was recommended in reviews by leading national publications. Her second book, *the Sun Always Rises* was written to help people recover and thrive in a time of loss.

Preface

Of Joy and Loneliness

In her new book the *Art of Connecting*, Kelly describes the joy of finding yourself again. What Kelly has discovered is that there is an epidemic of loneliness throughout the western world, but simply identifying it isn't enough. Rather than obsess about the condition, a wiser path is to focus on the cure: *the Art of Connecting*.

This book will help readers master the art of genuine connection, which turns out to also be the art of escaping loneliness and feeding your soul.

A good place to start is believing you are not as alone as you may think you are. What is your passion? What do you enjoy doing? What feeds your soul? These questions are guideposts to journeying out of loneliness and finding connection.

Kelly Lowe is a mother and grandmother—yes, sounds like a great life—but also a divorcee who has been widowed twice. She has faced many challenges in her life, including major surgeries. All of these experiences have led her to appreciate the kinds of peaks and valleys in her own life which we all encounter along our life's journey. She not only brings her life experience to her new book, but also those of others she's met and interviewed who have had to deal with feelings of loneliness and loss in their life. She shares the expertise of therapists she has interviewed who have worked with patients dealing with similar feelings.

And, as a professional Astrological Counselor, Motivational Speaker and Author, Kelly has counseled hundreds if not thousands of people to help them work through challenging cycles in their life. These experiences are part of what she "knows" and details in this new book.

In *An Astrologer's Journey* Kelly describes how astrology answered her youthful search for meaning and led her into a satisfying career as a nationally acclaimed astrology counselor. She has taught her workshops from Florida to California and points in between, and is known for intertwining a deep knowledge of human nature with suggestions for optimal timing according to the movements of the sun, moon, and planets.

Her monthly newsletter is available on her website at www.astrologytalk.com, and you can also visit her on Facebook.com/astrologytalk.com.

SECTION ONE

From The Heart ...

"You can't sing the blues unless you've had the blues." — BB King

This has not been an easy subject to write or talk about. Few of us want to admit that we are or were ever feeling lonely. It's like a personality flaw or something that we've done wrong. But what I have discovered is that almost everyone that I talked with during my research has experienced feeling lonely at one time or another in their life.

I've asked the questions: What is your passion? What do you enjoy doing? What feeds your soul? These are the questions that can lead to connection. If you don't have a passion, find one.

I find writing to be comforting and therapeutic—something I share with Elizabeth Gilbert. I wrote my first book, when my husband was diagnosed with cancer and my second book the year after he passed away. And now at the fourth anniversary of his passing I'm embracing the opportunity to share my research and experience about the feelings of loneliness and depression. My research has taught me that loneliness comes in many shapes and sizes. It doesn't have to be generated by a death or a divorce.

The passion that could lead you to connection may be something new in your life. I never really considered myself to be a writer when I was growing up, but I do find now that writing feeds my soul. (Although I always kept journals from the early age of 16, they were not for publication. I'm leaving strict instructions for my son to burn them upon my death. I would burn them myself if I knew what day that was going to be!)

I have found that what writing does is lead me into deeper, more honest evaluation of who I am and as a result makes me more comfortable with myself. I have grown to like myself and therefore being alone with "me" becomes a joyful experience.

Passions don't have to be discovered—like some God-given talent you had from birth but never knew about. They can be invented. Several women I know took up playing bridge to relieve boredom on a cruise. Now they can't get enough of it.

> **Surgeon General Rabec Morphy made headlines when he called loneliness an epidemic.**

You are not alone. Where have you heard that cliché before? Many people feel lonely when they have opportunities to connect but bypass them.

Have you ever wrestled with a problem, looked at it from every angle without finding a solution, and then all of a sudden understanding arrives pretty much gift-wrapped?

It wasn't until I was watching, *CBS News Good Morning, Sunday Morning* the Sunday before Valentine's Day, that I began to realize that my second book, *The Sun Always Rises, How to Thrive in Times Of Loss*, wasn't just about dealing with a death or a loss. It is also about dealing with loneliness and depression, although a death can certainly bring about the feeling of loneliness and depression. But you don't have to lose someone to experience those feelings. Perhaps, when I was writing that book, I wanted to show how one can make recovery happen, how to be optimistic in the darkest time. In so doing, I may have denied the extent to which I was feeling deep loneliness myself. I was not alone, but the person who helped make me feel complete was gone and it was natural that I should feel lonely.

Watching *CBS News Sunday Morning* that morning, I learned—also confirmed later during my interviews with psychologists and therapists—that approximately 60 percent of the population suffers from depression and or loneliness? Nearly half of all Americans say they feel lonely at one time or another. Surgeon General Rabec Morphy made headlines when he called loneliness an epidemic. He even said loneliness can be fatal. The increased mortality associated with feeling lonely is equal to the increased mortality of smoking 14 cigarettes a day and greater than the increased mortality associated with obesity.

Here's a phrase from the show that stuck in my mind: If you have four good friends, you are really lucky.

In the UK, loneliness is such a problem that the government has appointed a minister of loneliness. The Minister of Loneliness brings people together in short encounters—like talking over a cup of coffee, which may lead to longer meetings and over time, hopefully, to making a friend.

So, if we know about this widespread epidemic of loneliness in this country—that most everyone feels lonely at one time or another—the question becomes, what do we do about it?

First, we should recognize that to be lonely you do not have to be alone. It's not about the quantity of friends you have, or how busy you are. It is about the quality of the connection.

It doesn't matter how old you are. The conception is widespread that it is mainly older people who are lonely.

As it turns out, youth and younger adults may have a higher rate of loneliness—especially among Millennials, with the ever-present phone possibly partly at fault. Seeing an increase in social media use all around him, Dr. Brian A. Primack, MD, PhD, at the University of Arkansas, conducted a study he titled "Social Media Use and Perceived Social Isolation Among Young Adults in the U.S."

He concluded the more social media we use, the lonelier we are likely to be. Users can end up feeling they deserve to be lonely because, frankly, they simply aren't good enough. Facebook social comparisons often show only the good times and best pictures of the users. People feel they can't measure up with their normal life. Social media has contributed enormously to people feeling alone.

John Frances, a musician (banjo player) and mountain climber, was also interviewed for this Sunday morning show because he chose to stop talking on his 27th birthday and didn't say a word for 17 years. Now that he's "out," he believes in cultivating closeness selectively—having four really good friends is a blessing and much better than 4,000 Facebook likes.

John Frances asked, "Which is lonelier, to be with people that you are not communicating with, or to be by yourself?" The loneliest he ever felt was when he was with someone but still felt alone. He finally realized that being alone is not being lonely. As he was climbing a mountain, he realized he was not lonely. He was just alone. In his 70s, he is now an environmentalist, author and public speaker.

While the loneliness minister in the UK focused on leading people into friendships, another approach is learning to be mindful of the joy of being with yourself. Meditation is a great focusing and centering tool to get in touch with yourself, and leads to self-awareness.

You've probably heard it said that *wherever you go, there you are*. It may be a cliché, but it is true. However, the fact that we are eternally stuck with ourselves doesn't automatically mean that we know ourselves, or that we are comfortable with ourselves. This is an area where meditation can help. Feeling uncomfortable can lead us to hide from ourselves. This internal alienation, or confusion about who we are, can lead to a sense of absurdity about life itself. This feeling of separation doesn't need to be a lifelong event. It can be transient. Life has its twists and turns, and we can exit these stretches in a better place than where we went it. The Joy of finding ourselves again is what this book is all about.

The *CBS News Sunday Morning Show* also mentioned the moon and how it impacts people's emotions. The moon affects the ocean tides and our bodies are comprised of 75 percent water. So, the full moon is very powerful and impacts the way we feel and magnifies everything that is going on in our life. As an astrological counselor people come to me seeking personal guidance—not because they have problems with "the stars." While my life and work have taught me a great deal about human nature, my counseling does indeed incorporate knowledge of how the moon and planets affect our choices.

I will share more about the full moon later, but for now let me just say it puts things in our life under a microscope and forces us to see if we are happy with our life. You get clarity during the full moon. It's a time of self-analysis. It's a time to take personal inventory.

Finally, speaking of famous sayings and clichés, how about this one from BB King that I referenced at the beginning of this chapter: "You can't sing the blues unless you've had the blues." The Blues, as a musical form, is a way of publicly owning and even celebrating the hard times. Blues songs often are about being left alone when a spouse leaves you, but instead of moping, the blues singer takes it on full force—and with passion. I'm sure even BB King has felt lonely but singing the blues connects him with others who know what he's feeling. Together they can chase away the tears with smiles over their shared experience.

Section Two

CONNECTION AND LONELINESS
IN THE POPULAR CULTURE

We are so very connected in our culture through news media and social media, and yet connecting feels like a lost art. If you are feeling lonely and disconnected, you are not alone. The question is how to get connected. Our culture offers—sometimes sells—many possible ways to connect, but not all take you in the right direction. For example, people have actually connected through internet dating but it brings its own risks for isolating us. What will work for you? We experiment. We find our passion, but maybe not on the first try. There are no guarantees. Even the celebrities so admired in our culture face the same challenge—despite living lives filled with other people.
Connecting is an art we can learn, but it's an active art. In some ways loneliness is a call to action.

"Everybody's On The Phone So Connected And All Alone"

I am a firm believer that everyone and everything comes into our life at the perfect time. As I was on my way to meet a friend for lunch one day, this song came on the radio by Jimmy Buffett. Of course, anyone who knows me knows that I am a die hard "Parrott Head" and have my Sirius Radio set on the Jimmy Buffett channel. Although I don't remember hearing this song in a long time it never resonated with me as it did on that day, when I was in the process of writing this book.

It was the same message from a different source that was validating and saying the same thing that the therapists and doctors had shared with me during our interviews. I found it to be very interesting that Jimmy Buffett had also figured this out.

In his song, "Everybody's on The Phone," he described the situation perfectly. In fact, my research tells me the problem has metastasized and become an even greater contributor to feelings of loneliness since 2008 when the song was first released.

Message in a bottle
Rhythm of a drum
Smoke signals and telegraphs
Make the airwaves hum

But that's all ancient history
Like bongs and Lincoln Logs
Now we livin' like the Jet sons
In a wacky wireless fog

Now we livin' like the Jet sons
In a wacky wireless fog

Talkin', squawkin', hawkin'
Who knows if anybody's gettin' through

We act like crazy people
Talking to ourselves
Crashing cars in conversation
Still that shit flies off the shelf

The information superhighways
Crawled up like a L.A. traffic jam

Everybody's on the phone
So connected and all alone

From the pizza boy to the socialite
We all salute the satellites

Won't you text me with your master plan?
You're loud and clear but I don't understand
I'm a digital explorer in analog roam
And everybody's on the phone

Do you remember dialing up?
Yes, I remember well
Now I just can't go anywhere
Without my sacred cell

I think that I might die
If I miss anything at all
Text me, send me an e-mail
Ring me up, give me a call

I'm ADD on AOL and tryin' to read
The writing on the wall
And I'm a digital explorer in an analog roam
And everybody's on the phone

(Written by Jimmy Buffett, Peter Hagen Mayer, Roger Guth, Will Kimbrough • Copyright © BMG Rights Management)

I don't know about you, but I could really relate to this song. It brought everything into perspective for me. And this was written before Facebook and Instagram were so ramped.

This song also reminded me of my retreat in Hawaii, which I'll will talk more about later. We had no internet or cell service for one week. That was an amazing withdrawal experience—excruciating at first but eventually a blessing. The interesting thing was that it didn't take me long to fall back into my old habits once I hit the mainland and returned home. In retrospect, I feel sad about that and realize that the obsession with the need to stay connected is not always a good thing. It can be a difficult habit to break. For some it is more difficult than others.

I believe identifying the problem and making a conscious decision is a big step. How do you feel when you are out of touch? Does it bother you?

I am always reminded of this feeling during hurricane season. Living in Florida during hurricane season is always interesting. The first thing we usually loose is our power. The internet goes down. And sometimes the cell towers are down. I've even thought of sending smoke signals. The longest I've had to endure this torture was two weeks. This was a good exercise for being disconnected, although not one that I would intentionally choose. The interesting thing is that it doesn't take long to get back to our old habits and addictions. Yes, I used the word addictions because my research has shown that social medial and the need to stay connected can be an addiction, and it can lead to the feeling of loneliness.

Sex And The City

"They Went Clubbing Every Night Looking For A Connection"

As I was doing research for this book, I took a break and became addicted to the classic series, *Sex in The City*. This was a signature HBO comedy series starring Jessica Parker as a thirtysomething writer whose personal life and friendships are source material for her weekly column. It's about how young or not so young single women and men meet the challenge of finding a mate?

You may recall Carrie Bradshaw, a journalist who wrote a sex column for a New York Magazine; Samantha, who had a public relations business; Maranda, the successful attorney; and Charlotte, the aspiring artist. These women were very successful in their careers but still they were hungry for connection in their friendship with each other.

They went clubbing together every night unless one of them had a hot date. They were always window shopping. They were always looking for a romantic connection. This was long before dating online became popular. Maybe someone should do another series about that. But, wait someone did! It was called *Dirty John*.

In *Sex in The City* everyone was worried about being along and never meeting the right man. Of course, we know that is not the answer to never feeling lonely. What a myth that was. I know so many married people that are lonely.

I don't think I really appreciated the show as much during its first run in 1998 as I did when I binged watched it on Amazon Prime. Amazon is becoming my new best friend—just kidding. I really don't watch that much TV. Little did we know then that it would be a classic and the relevance that it would have to the loneliness epidemic that we are experiencing in today's culture. There is a desire to connect now just as there was in 90s. There was the clubbing and girlfriend bonding. And lord knows they all worked very hard at supplying Carrie with material for her column.

I guess I would be Carrie, the writer, looking for Mr. Big. But then haven't we all been looking for our Mr. Big at one time or another in our life. Many of us still are, although we know that true happiness comes from within. I just wish I had Carrie's job, although I know that I could not keep up with that night life or wearing the four-inch heels.

An Inspiration from Dolly Parton

What do you love to do?
What makes your life a little brighter?

I have always enjoyed Dolly Parton's music and appreciated her talent, so when *CBS Sunday Morning* was interviewing her, my ears perked up and I took out my note pad. (As I have mentioned before, I am a big *CBS Sunday Morning* fan.) Dolly shared that she works way more than "9 to 5"—as in her hit song and movie. It's more like 24 – 7. She said "it's my therapy."

"My guitar is my friend," she said. "When I'm in that zone, I call it my 'God zone', I love that time." When people ask her why don't you retire, she says, "and do what? I count my blessing more than I do my dollars. It's the art. I love to work."

She has sold more than a hundred million albums. She was the fourth of twelve children. She said music always made everything a little brighter. She said she could write songs at an early age. She was about 10 when she started writing. She has written more than 3,000 songs. And she is funny as a hoot. No wonder I have always liked her.

Dolly Parton is an American singer, songwriter, multi-instrumentalist, record producer, actress, author, businesswoman, and humanitarian, known primarily for her work in country music.

Patrick Swayze

Still Hungry for Connection

Does being hungry for connection, mean you are fighting off loneliness or depression? You'd think a person who is as busy as Patrick Swayze would have plenty to feed on. And why could someone with all the connections of a Hollywood star still be hungry?

But as I was watching *Entertainment Tonight* one evening they started talking about Patrick Swayze, who I dearly love, and I was very surprised to hear that he had a hunger for connection. He made it known by reaching out to people with everything he did.

When he filmed *Dirty Dancing*, he said he was going to put all his battles over human relations out there—at every opportunity. This is good to know. It's one more way of knowing that even if we are feeling lonely, "we are not alone."

Let your words and actions speak: yes, I too am hungry for connection. You are likely to find more kindred spirits than you guessed. I was also surprised to learn that Patrick Swayze had an alcohol problem. I don't doubt the two things are related, but that is a subject for another time.

The Lure and Promise of Internet Dating

*Internet dating ... an illusion
or a solution for loneliness?*

Although dating online can certainly fill your time, it can also contribute to loneliness. This road can be paved with disappointments. If you're going to go down this road it helps if you are in the right frame of mind. First, you can't take rejection personally. You can't expect instant results or to immediately meet the love of your life. This is not for the faint of heart.

While doing my research one woman experienced with internet dating told me there are no Prince Charmings or Snow Whites waiting on the internet dating sites.

The other thing that my research has warned about is getting caught up in a scam for money. When people are lonely and searching for a connection there may be a tendency to be vulnerable and want to see and believe the best in people. The stories these scam artists have told can be heart breaking and sound true, but, really, just say "no" and see how long the connection lasts.

In all fairness this is not about doom and gloom. I have heard of many people who have met their spouses online. I'm just saying, it is not for everyone. You have to be clear and concise in your mind, and in your understanding of what you are looking for.

Of course, this goes back to the reality that no one can make you happy. Peace and happiness come from within and a relationship is a complement not a solution.

NEIGHBORS HELPING NEIGHBORS

Connecting After A Hurricane Or Natural Disaster

Necessity is the Mother of Invention

When you live in a hurricane prone state you know that hurricanes and everything that swirls around them—like preparing for them and following their path—are a shared part of the popular culture. If you are looking for an opportunity to connect, there's nothing like a hurricane to bring people together. Of course we also pray that the storm will pass us by, but it's amazing how people band together and support each other in times of a disaster or an impending disaster. Even estranged neighbors, family members and friends come together and form a bond to support and help each other in a time of need. It is a true example of connecting. It's sad that it sometimes takes this to bring people back together again, but it's great that it does.

Then there is the letdown and readjustment after the storm passes, when everyone goes back to their normal routine and the feeling of connection can be lost. Was it just a crisis connection? That can be depressing. It requires a conscious effort to stay connected after the crises has passed.

Since I live in Florida in hurricane alley, I have experienced this feeling of connection and disconnection firsthand many times. I can recall one hurricane a few years ago—I believe it was Matthew—when we lost cable services for five days. Keep in mind that my cable service is a bundle package that includes TV, WIFI internet, and my landline. Although I was thrilled that I did not lose my electric, you would think that someone had cut off my oxygen supply when I did not have these services.

Yes, I was thrilled that I still had air conditioning, lights, a hot shower, a stove, microwave, and the elevator in my building, which was still running. But no internet or TV, what's a girl to do? This gave the feeling of being disconnected a whole new meaning. Of course, now I would embrace the situation as an opportunity to write. But as I recall, I did manage to get caught up on a lot of reading and home projects. It turned out to be a very introspective and productive time in my life, a time that I will never forget. Hindsight is always better than the reality.

Even if you don't live in hurricane ally, I invite you to take some time to think about what you would do if you lost your internet connection to the outside world for five days. Some people choose to do this when they take a cruise, but they are being entertained and enjoying new sights. You might want to try this exercise of disconnecting with the outside world, especially if you live alone. I guarantee it will give you a whole different perspective and help you get connected with yourself.

Section Three

NATURAL GIFTS TO FEED THE SOUL

Yoga, meditation, Reiki, Biofield Tuning, conscious eating, Qigong, use of essential oils, and regular exercise are all practices which bring us in touch with both our physical and spiritual self. They lead us toward peace and connection with others. These practices are all tools that I have found to be very helpful.

Yoga And Connection
by Krista Oakes, Yoga Instructor, E-RYT

The Yoga Class is Only the Beginning

Yoga is a wonderful tool for connection! When people come together with other like-minded people to do something positive and good for themselves it's inevitable that community is built, relationships are formed, and compassion and understanding is felt.

I have been teaching yoga for over fifteen years and I owned a formal yoga studio for five of those years. That studio became like a community center where people could come together, count on seeing someone they knew, and be asked about if they didn't show up.

Time spent together often extends way beyond the yoga class. A yoga community of any size or kind offers a reason to get up in the morning and a place to go to be with other people doing something positive for both the body and the mind.

However, with yoga the connection goes even deeper because its also establishes a deeper connection with yourself. The whole goal of yoga is to practice awareness so that in any given time we can be present and conscious in the present moment. A mindfulness practice means spending less time in the past or in the future, neither of which we have any control over. Through the breath and posture work done on a yoga mat, we learn to set everything else aside, to let everything just fade in to the background (stress, worries, thoughts, aches and pains) and instead direct all our awareness within ourselves. With this focus on the self we become intimately familiar with our own body, emotions, and tendencies. When we let go of the past and the future and stay in the present, we are naturally more content, happy, compassionate, kind, and the list goes on. When we are open and content, connection happens!

Yoga is a mindfulness practice that offers a plethora of benefits from physical health to emotional health. It alleviates aches and pain and allows us to heal from injuries and slow down aging. It helps to reduce stress, anxiety, and depression. It improves our mood, and creates discipline and overall awareness. And it is a practice that most definitely leads us to connection with others and perhaps, more importantly, ourselves.

Another Tool To Help Along The Road

What is Reiki and How Does it Work?

Reiki can help with stress, headaches, insomnia, upset stomachs, sprains and other minor ailments. It also promotes psychological healing including release of anger, fear, sadness, grief and other unhealthy feeling. It also helps with PTSD and has been used in hospitals and VA Medical Centers throughout the country. It is used as a compliment to Western medicine. That is why it is called a form of Complementary Medicine. Reiki does not treat illness; it balances your energy and puts you in a state of deep relaxation so your body can heal itself.

After experiencing several treatments, I found it to be a very helpful tool in my toolbox to help during times of stress and back pain. When I asked my Reiki practitioner, Mary Chereskin RN, MSN how this all worked and what it was about, she shared this information with me from the International Center for Reiki training.

There is an unseen energy flow through all living things that affects the quality of a person's health. Some cultures call it chi and some call it Ki. The word Reiki is really two words. Rei means universal and Ki means life force energy, so Reiki balances your life force energy

If the flow of Ki is interrupted, physical organs and tissues will be adversely affected. This is the main cause of illness. When your energy is low you are more susceptible to illness, it is more difficult to deal with stress and you may not sleep well. Reiki is a technique that increases a person's supply of life force energy.

Developed in Japan in 1922, it is a form of energy healing that balances the mind, body and spirit. The practitioner's hands hover over or lightly touch the client. The practitioner may lay hands on various areas of your body, but the energy will go to the area where it is most needed. You may notice sensations where the practitioner's hands are, maybe heat or subtle movement. Areas of your body will become more open and feel more comfortable. If you have pain it will likely diminish.

Reiki allows the muscles to relax and the blood to flow to the treated area, which helps the healing process.

A Reiki session is usually performed on a massage table and usually lasts about 45 to 60 minutes. You remain fully clothed. There are no adverse effects from a Reiki session.

To learn more visit the International Center for Reiki training at reiki.org or pick up a copy of *Reiki, A Compressive Guide* by Pamela Miles (2006).

"And if I'm alone when night falls, I will go to the window, look up at the sky and feel certain that loneliness is a lie, because the universe is there to keep me company."
— Paulo Chehelo, Author of "The Alchemist"

Biofield Tuning

"Stay tuned for Living"

When a friend invited me to attend a talk and demonstration about an alternative treatment for healing and helping us deal with anxiety, loneliness and depression, I was intrigued to learn more. And I wasn't disappointed. Although I wasn't feeling well that night and almost declined the invitation, I was very happy that I went.

Iris Sandove, a Certified Biofield Practitioner, shared this information in her very organized and enlightening presentation.

Biofield Tuning is a unique non-medical, therapeutic modality. The practitioner uses tuning forks on and around the body to locate and correct distortions in the body's energy field. This work has the capability for tremendous transformation in a person's life. This form of vibrational healing helps remove old stuck patterns and behaviors impeding you from living your highest and best. It tunes up the body's energy system, restoring balanced energetic wholeness. Biofield Tuning has the capacity to clear old traumas that are still present in the energy field and continue to influence the present.

With the use of turning forks she can locate stagnant energy and move it back into the body. Subconscious blocks can be removed helping to release stress and anxiety. This cutting-edge, sound science is effective in quieting the nervous system. The coherent vibrations of the tuning forks work to shift the energy around painful memories, and old beliefs. Through the therapeutic applications of sound, stress is released and the body relaxes. This simple non-invasive and effective method can produce profound and powerful outcomes on multiple levels.

Iris's presentation also described the symptoms that are treated successfully with Biofield Tuning, which I found to be very convincing. I immediately related it to the research I was doing as I was writing this book.

Those symptoms include:
- Pain
- Anxiety
- PTSD
- Adrenal Stress
- Digestive Issued
- Depression
- Fibromyalgia
- Addictions

- Panic Attacks
- Vertigo
- Migraines/headaches
- Restless Leg Syndrome
- "Stuckness" and much more....

She also said people have a yearning for a sense of connection because we live in an environment where everything is perceived as separate and separated, which I found to be very though provoking.

Iris Sandove can be reached online at staytunedforliving.com or by email at staytuned16@yahoo.com.

After listening to Iris's presentation, I was immediately drawn to schedule an appointment with her for a treatment and once again, I was not disappointed. I found it to be everything she described: relaxing, therapeutic and healing.

What You Eat Can Determine How You Feel

Eating Your Way to Mental Health

Have you ever thought about how what you eat can affect the way you feel? It wasn't until I was watching the wide-ranging special on CBS Sunday Morning that the concept started resonating with me. And it made a lot of sense. I can remember when I was on my Qigong retreat in Hawaii and they emphasized the importance of a healthy colorful diet, but I didn't at that time connect it with a treatment for depression or anxiety.

Globe trotting photographer, David Kruqman, said he felt at home no matter where he went and had 3,000+ Instagram followers but said he was still not happy. He wasn't enjoying his day-to-day life. He tried therapy and antidepressants without success. Then an unconventional psychologist, Dr. Drew Ramsey, posed an unconventional question to Krugman. He asked him what he ate. And when he thought about what he was eating it really opened his eyes.

This is when he was introduced to nutritional psychiatry. He began to eat what is often called the

Mediterranean diet—colorful vegetables, seafood, olive oil and lots of leafy greens.

Dr. Ramsey also said that oysters are one of the best foods for depression and said his work has proven very conclusively that what you eat impacts the way you feel.

He said the idea that we can just take supplements and be healthy is simply not true. The proof is in the pictures when you look at a brain scan of someone who has followed the Mediterranean diet verses a high fat, hi-carb diet.

Also mentioned in this CBS Sunday morning special was that The Washington Post published an article about new research that links diet and mental health called "For brain health, skip the supplements and focus on a healthy diet." Here is the link:

https://www.washingtonpost.com/health/for-brain-health-skip-the-supplements-and-focus-on-a-healthy-diet/2019/06/28/885b61b4-9837-11e9-916d-9c61607d8190_story.html

What motivates us to do what we do? For me it is the desire to stay mentally and physically healthy and stay independent.

Exercise: The Multi-Purpose Therapy

The Many Benefits of Staying Fit

Exercise and physical activities have always played a major role in my life. Sometimes it plays a more prominent role than other times, but it's always been at the top of my list of things to make time for. So when going through stressful or distressful times I kick it into high gear.

When my husband Larry passed away in 1993, I started training for mini triathlons with my son. It really helped me stay connected and fight off feelings of depression.

I believe it was a saving grace for me. It helped me to move forward physically and emotionally. People will say that it's "good to stay busy and take your mind off it," but it's more than that. There's something about movement of the muscles, especially the large muscles, that has its own magic. It gets the endorphins and adrenalin going.

It can be euphoric and mentally healing. At least I have always found it be.

Then in 2015 when my husband Tony passed away, I decided to join a second gym. I had been a member of the YMCA for years because they had an Olympic pool which I loved. I felt that I was ready to step up my workout with additional activities that the other gym offered. And besides, moving into a new environment felt very appealing.

I knew that triathlons were no longer in my future, due to some physical limitations, but I could still swim, spin, do yoga, and ride my bike on the beach.

During those days of recovery in the first year after, swimming attracted me more than any of the others. After all, it was impossible to cry while I was swimming, so I swam a lot. And since swimming is one of the best exercises you can do for your body, I was loving it. There's no stress on your body when you're in the water.

Swimming seems to always be there as the perfect exercise. It was the very first thing that I could get back to doing when I was recovering from hip replacement and quadriceps surgeries. Of course I didn't have these surgeries at the same time.

I could actually swim before I could walk after I had my quadriceps reattached to my knee bone. That was fun. Fortunately, Tony was still with me during that time. Although he was not Nancy nurse, he did the best he could, which was to call my aunt and uncle in California to come stay with us.

Fortunately, I was a fast healer and bounced back quickly from my surgeries. I expected, or at the very least, hoped to bounce back emotionally after my husband passed away. But broken hearts seem to take longer to mend then hips and knees do. I know that now.

Extra "bennies" from staying fit and working out

What motivates us to do what we do? For me it is the desire to stay mentally and physically healthy—the desire to maintain my independence until I am at least 101 so that my son and/or grandchildren do not need to take care of me.

It's the desire to stay healthy so that I can live and work as much as possible with compassion for others. Helping is why I chose my profession and why I write. I recommend it as a motivation in life. Of course, you never know when your opportunity will come to influence someone in a small but positive way.

So yes, working out was fun for me and when it brought me a little notoriety in my hometown I had to smile. The Community Editor from our local paper interviewed me for a special interest feature about "working out and staying young." I share it here with you in hopes of expressing my desire to see just one more person start on a path to fitness.

**Work Out, Stay Young:
That's The Kelly Lowe Way**

Emily Blackwood, Community Editor for the Ormond Beach Observer
Every day, Kelly Lowe has a different plan. On Monday and Wednesday she swims for 45 minutes. She rides the stationary bike at Gold's Gym Tuesday and Thursday and then takes a

yoga class.

And on Friday, she plays golf. "I do something active every day," she said. "And golf definitely counts."

During the weekend, the Ormond Beach resident keeps up her routine with something a little more low key, like a walk on the beach. It is the weekend after all.

"I've always tried to stay physically active," Lowe-Pirkle said with a smile. "Varying exercise makes sure my body doesn't get overworked."

For those who are just starting out, the lifelong astrologist and published author says to start off with doing one activity that you like just two days a week. Rather than form this big fitness plan, make small goals that you know you can easily attain. That will keep you motivated to do more.

When it comes to eating healthy, Lowe-Pirkle advocates for staying away from sugars. She advises to eat low-carb foods.

"I try to stay away from sugar," she said. "Not that I don't have wine, but wine doesn't count."

Her diet consist of a lot of veggies, fruits and proteins. She says salmon and celery are some of the best things you could eat.

While the motivation to stay consistent with a healthy lifestyle can sometimes be hard to maintain, Lowe-Pirkle said she does so because it keeps her feeling young and energetic.

"You're going to be able to think better," she said. "Your attitude is going to be better. It's your state of mind that is so rewarding."

I must say that this article certainly gave me an added boost and inspired me to continue my regimen, which has served me well. My commitment to exercise has not only helped me to move forward emotionally it has helped me to stay strong, fit and healthy.

You don't have to be a triathlete or even join a gym. Any regular form of exercise can be mentally and physically healing and helpful. Even a walk around the block can lift your spirits and help your attitude. Ask yourself, "What is the one thing I can do right now, given who I am and the resources I have?" Do that one thing, then go a step further from there.

A SOURCE OF ENERGY TO LIFT BODY, MIND AND SPIRIT

Another case in point that comes to mind is a gentleman I met after his wife of many years passed away. He shared with me that he had put on a lot of extra pounds while he was caring for her during her extended illness. His cholesterol was high. His blood pressure was high, and he got absolutely no exercise. His diet was, to put it simply, atrocious. He was on a fast track for disaster. Then he became motivated and interested in swimming laps in the pool. Five laps a day was all he could handle the first week.

After a few months he was up to twenty laps. He could see and feel the excess pounds melting away just by changing his diet and incorporating swimming into his daily routine. Not only did he look better, he said he felt so much better. He was healthier. He had more energy. His anxiety and depression started to subside. He was beginning to feel and look like a new person. In fact, he was a new person. He dropped three sizes in his pants and went from an extra-large to medium shirt size.

Then he decided to join the gym and work out on the treadmill and weight machines. He even joined a Yoga class. He was embracing his new self. He loved this new source of energy that seemed to feed his body and mind and lift his spirits. As his exercise regimen increased, his oxygen flow also seemed to increase. He was on a roll and he loved it. The last time I spoke with him he had lost over 50 lbs. He said he felt great and was enjoying the compliments. He was physically and mentally a new and different person. More importantly, he was, once again, a person he liked and enjoyed being.

Exercise can be a wonderful tool, good for so many things including renewing your enthusiasm for life. It can certainly help us enjoy the sunrises during a morning walk—if you can get up early. Put your faith in knowing that whatever your pain, the sun will rise in the morning and you will be given the blessing of another day.

Essential Oils To Help With Depression

Ancient Therapy Remains Affective Today

I was pleasantly surprised when my niece introduced me to essentials oils as I was going through a very rough time. She said they can be used as a remedy for almost everything and anything, from depression, insomnia, arthritis to bug bite,. just to name a few of the remedies.

I discovered that essential oils, known as nature's living energy, are the natural, aromatic volatile liquids found in shrubs, flower, trees, roots, bushes, and seeds. The distinctive components in essential oils defend plants against insects, sentimental conditions, and disease. They are also vital for plants to grow, live, evolve, and adapt to their surroundings. Essential oils are extracted from aromatic plant sources via steam distillation and are highly concentrated and far more potent than dry herbs.

While essential oils often have a pleasant aroma, their chemical makeup is complex and their benefits vast—which makes them much more than something that simply smells good.

Historical Use of Essential Oils

Historically, essential oils have played a prominent role in everyday life. With more than 200 references to aromatics, incense and ointment throughout the Bible, essential oils are said to be used for anointing and healing the sick. Today, essential oils are used for aromatherapy, massage therapy, emotional health, personal care, nutritional supplements, household solutions, and much more.

Essential oils are considered mankind's first medicine and have been used around the world for centuries. Essential oils and other aromatics have been used in religious rituals, to help support the body's natural systems, and for other physical and spiritual needs.

Research dates the use of essential oils back to 4500 B.C. Ancient Egyptians were the first to discover the potential of fragrances and records demonstrate that the Egyptians of antiquity used oils and aromatics for treating illness as well as performing rituals and religious ceremonies in temples, and for burial rites discovered by archeologists exploring the pyramids.

According to ancient Egyptian hieroglyphics and Chinese manuscripts, priests and physicians used oils thousands of years before the time of Christ. There are more than 188 references to oils in the Bible, and some precious oils like Frankincense, Myrrh, Rosemary, Cassia, and Cinnamon were used for the anointing and healing of the sick.

As with anything in life, when the student is ready the teacher appears. My niece was there at just the right time to introduce these amazing healing tools to me. She mixed a magic potion to help me sleep better and to elevate my mood and sense of happiness within, which is why I have added essential oils to my research when writing this book.

(Reference: Young Living Essential Oils , Life Science Quick Reference Tool)

Be diligent in your practice. Whatever it may be—Qigong, Tai chi, Yoga, Meditation or some other form—do it several times a week.

Spiritual Practice And The Art Of Connecting
Harnessing The Energy That Feeds Your Soul

In a later chapter I will describe in more detail a week-long Qigong retreat in Hawaii, which was my turning point toward recovery, or rebirth after my husband's passing. It is one of the "natural gifts" available to us for feeding our souls.

Many of us have uplifting experiences at seminars or retreats that may last no more than a weekend, or a week at most. The question is how to take that elevated feeling you leave with you and make it real every day of your life. How do you make it last? The answer, I believe, is you need to have a practice whatever it may be. It could be Qigong, Tai chi, yoga, one of the many forms of meditation, or even prayer. Do it daily or at least several times a week. It may not blow your socks off like a week in Hawaii, but the cumulative effect will be greater for bringing joy and peace of mind into your life.

Qigong is a lifestyle that harnesses energy from

special movements, breathing methods and uses specific foods to reverse specific diseases. Everyone has a healing hand and anyone can benefit with practice.*

I came across this quote from Dr. Rick Agel MD and AP Surgeon of Atlanta, Georgia, about the Qigong system I leaned in Hawaii. "This system combines Qigong with Breathing Exercises that are *phenomenally energetic.* In thirty years of practicing Tai Chi, this is the strongest chi I've ever felt."

So, when my friend Krista invited me to a weekend Qigong forum I went full of anticipation, but not knowing exactly what to expect. Believe me when I say that I was not disappointed. It was exactly what I needed. I was introduced into a whole new world of personal empowerment.

I have been practicing yoga and meditating for years. I went through the Transcendental Meditation course when I was going through my divorce in the 70s. I thought I was an experienced and seasoned meditator, but I had never experienced the serene feeling that Qigong gave me. It was even better than a couple glasses of wine or a martini. I would come home at night after a full day and evening of practicing and absorbing this new discipline, feeling a sense of a euphoric high.

I did not need or want to turn on the TV or even listen to music. I experienced a feeling of serenity and introspection. I was truly in touch with my healing journey. I was in a good place.

The weekend was not only about physical and mental exercise it was about nutrition and healthy eating. It was about feeding the mind, body and spirit—which, as it turned, out was exactly what I needed to help me on my healing journey at that time in my life.

People use the word "holistic" quite freely, but when one really practices with a thought to all parts of your being—mind, body and spirit—it brings a peace through internal unity that can't be reached when one part of the equation is missing.

I am always amazed at how, when we take one brave step forward, the universe takes our hand and walks with us. As Julia Cameron, author of *the Artist's Way*, likes to say, "Leap and the net will appear." The weekend retreat in Daytona Beach was an invitation to leap, and I did by signing up for the week in Hawaii.

After my husband passed away I continued working with my astrology clients and helping other people with the challenges in their life. I continued teaching and scheduling workshops. I continued to stay busy and keep my mind occupied, but since I was still healing and adjusting to the loss of my husband, I felt I needed this opportunity, this retreat, to work on myself and regain my inner peace and strength. I say *regain*, which I think most people who've suffered loss hope for. The surprise waiting was for me was that I was destined not only to regain my former self, but to surpass the person I was before.

Section Four

WHAT HEALERS SAY ABOUT
LONELINESS AND CONNECTION

As I spoke with therapists and counselors in the mental health field, it became clear that loneliness and the feeling of being disconnected can prevent us from living truly joyful lives. Each interview was different, and so the form of each story also differs. You will hear something new from each of the professionals that I interviewed, although similar ideas come up time and again throughout the interviews as each counselor or therapist speaks about their experiences.

> *"I think it's true what they say: Life really is a journey—and it's not always easy to know which maps to trust, or what to pack for the trip. But whatever the weather, wherever the road leads, I think the best possible traveling advice would be this: Bring a friend."*
> — Keely Chace

Dr. Valerie Watt
Superficial Connections Just Don't Work

When I spoke with mental health professional Dr. Valerie Watt, our main focus was about loneliness. She said she was not surprised to hear that over 60 percent of the population has felt lonely at one time or another. She believes that the shift in the way people live today and not living near their families or family origins is a contributing factor. No one takes the time to connect with other people because people have left their origins behind and don't congregate anymore. She used the example of people moving from up north to Florida.

This is especially true for the elderly living alone. When people relocate there is often no person-to-person, face-to-face sense of community bonding.

They feel more bonded with people through

social media even though they are far way. This, she suggested, is a false sense of friendship.

Facebook connections are superficial by nature. People are feeling a disconnect from each other because they are not bonding like they were accustomed to in their earlier life. Dr. Watt said people are simply not developing friendships like they did when she was growing up.

She has seen people getting involved with the wrong romantic partner just because they are desperate to fill in the void that is not being met, which unfortunately only adds to the feeling of loneliness. They are bouncing from one person to the next, just because they are so desperate to fill their emotional void, which ends up being only a temporary fix. If there is no real emotional bonding they move on. Dr. Watt stressed again that physical attraction and hormones only last so long.

Dr. Watt said it is important for women to develop a network of female friendships. It takes work and effort but many things work to prevent it: We have become emotionally lazy, other things get in the way, or people with whom friendships already existed no longer live as close to each other as they had.

She feels it's harder to build friendships in Florida. She suggested as a solution to join groups as they can become your default network and friends.

"Pick a couple of different things that you are interested in and join the group and if you're lucky you'll find a best friend or two," she said.

Dr. Katherine M. Billiot
A Correlation Between Internet Access and Loneliness

My interview with Dr. Katherine M. Billiot, Psy.D., was more wide ranging and touched on ways our culture works against people trying to make connections that will bring light to the darkness. She brought some very enlightening—and affirming—validations to the surface.

How does Social Media contribute to feelings of loneliness and depression?

"Social media is a tool that people can use to increase connectivity, but it can also create the need for constant validation by documenting everything we do, what you had for lunch, your surgery, etc. But it is missing the human energy and connection as you get with a face to face personal social environment."

Dr. Billiot shared with me that "there is a strong correlation between internet access and loneliness. Social media is one of the biggest issues which create a need for constant validation."

I asked Dr. Billiot what her advice would be for

a patient who complains of loneliness?

Her response: "Make the effort to get out of the house. Some people won't go out and meet people. They stay on their computer and the internet. No one is going to hand you a support group.

"You don't have to be old to be lonely. The dynamics are different for younger people than older. The younger folks are used to friends on Instagram and social media and don't *seem* to need the human connection as much.

"Many people no longer have the church connection, the congregation, the block party. Loneliness seems to decrease with a church and congregation connection."

I followed up by asking her how you get a connection? Not everyone who joins a church or another group finds one.

She said it won't happen if involvement remains on the surface. "It's not enough to take one yoga class and expect to get connected. It must be something like a four-week cooking class or an eight-week writing course—something that is repeated, something where you have a common interest with a consistent schedule. Join a book club, or a support group.

Being in the presence of other people is important but ...

"You can be in a group of people and still be lonely. It is about connecting with people. Loneliness isn't about being with people, it's about intimacy. It's not about sex. Some people have sex to escape loneliness. Unless you have a connection, that doesn't work.

"Filling the loneliness with sex is not the

answer. You can have sex and still be lonely and a lot of people are. That is not healthy. It's about shared values, shared interests."

She told me the story of a woman who had an illness and said her husband adored her and did everything for her, and still she felt lonely.

"What are your expectations? People who are married can still feel lonely. At the end of the day, you are still 'me, myself and I' in your head. No matter how many friends and family members you have supporting you, you still have to figure out a way to be happy with yourself. No one else is in your head. You have to be good company to yourself. You can have a whole audience of people with you supporting your feelings, but we are all born alone and die alone.

"Appreciate the connections when you have them, but when we are alone, are you good company for yourself? That's a part of the key."

What we can learn from Bohemian Rhapsody.

"The movie *Bohemian Rhapsody* was a perfect example of dealing with loneliness. Poor Freddie. People think being famous keeps you from being lonely. That's not true. They have folks around them that are just clinging to them for what they have and not who they are as an individual.  The rock star (Freddie Mercury) leaves the stage and his loneliness overpowers him. Being with people doesn't mean you're not lonely. It's about quality not quantity. This is not only true for rock stars but for everyone. Elton John is another good example who fought desperate loneliness in his early days when he aspired to fame and fortune."

I keep going back to the statement I heard on the *CBS News Good Morning Sunday* show that made me appreciate that I do have four good friends and motivated me to write this book: *"If you have four good friends in your life you are very fortunate. It's better than having 4,000 face book friends. It's about intimacy and sharing."* I have heard this statement affirmed repeatedly by everyone I talked to, and Dr. Billiot was no exception.

"I would take four good friends over anything. Relationships are like plants—we must nurture them, which takes time.

"The need for immediate, instant gratification has increased. Shopping online and the easy access to the internet gives people the notion that everything is instant gratification. Friends don't happen that way but we expect the same with friends, which leads to disappointment. Friends must be cultivated. People don't have as much patience to build intimacy and friendships in this day and age. And there's internet dating. That, she said, is another story, and we touched on it only briefly.

"If dating, and the first two months are not good, it isn't likely to get any better. Romantic relationships should be relatively easy, but romantic relationship isn't the answer to overcoming loneliness."

I'm busy and have a lot of friends, so why do I feel lonely?

When I asked Dr. Billiot how she would

The Art of Connecting 61

respond to a patient who came to her with this question she said, "Loneliness is complicated. You can be too busy to connect. Slow down and be in the moment. Smell the roses. Cultivating stillness. We have to work to be calm and present and still. The internet does not cultivate stillness; it is a time sucker. That's ok if it's a conscious choice. People want to see things in black and white, the internet is bad. It's okay, if you do it with conciseness. It's like eating chocolate. Don't eat too much chocolate. You don't want to be fat. Be mindful. Playing games on the internet is the same. Be more mindful of where your time and focus is spent. Be more deliberate about how you spend your time. Learn how to be in the moment. All healing roads lead to mindfulness."

She then shared something she had been thinking about.

"Assuming we are part of the animal species, we have fleshy bodies and bones, a nervous system through which we are wired for survival. We are wired to be aware of dangerous threats. Our bodies physiologically react to dangerous threats. Happiness is not the default. Cavemen did not have to be happy to have babies and multiply. If anything, a little bit of anxiety is the default, because that's what keeps us alive. Think about how the cavemen instinctively survived. Happiness is not the default. Anxiety is the default. The way to counteract that natural survival wiring is to be mindful of the moment we are in.

"We must be mindful to be happy and joyful. Be mindful of the moment we are in. A perfect example of not being mindful is to be with people who are not really present. They are texting, connecting superficially with people who are not physically present as biological beings. How often have you seen families and friends at a restaurant all with their phone out instead of interacting with each other?" she asked.

"Put the damn phone down and spend time together. The social pressure is to be available by phone or internet. Checking our email five times a day does not make you more productive. It makes you less productive. Every minute of the day is a precocious minute you can't get back.

"People are tied to their email."

Her research as shown that this constant digital "checking in," which some claim as a necessity, in fact makes you less productive. She suggested going on a cruise and disconnecting from your phone. She said she is not going to lose herself to technology. Some people's egos are wrapped up in their phones and how busy they are. "I'll bet those people are quite lonely," she said. "If you are busy all the time you are not present. If we do nothing some of us feel anxiety.

"People hate cruises because they must pay for the internet and they feel disconnected, when in fact they are already disconnected." She said she only checks her email every three days, which ironically is the time it takes for a piece of "snail mail" to arrive!

"The difference between being miserable and being happy takes conscious effort," Dr. Billiot said. "If you are busy all the time you are not present. If we do nothing some of us feel anxiety."

When she asks people, "What activities or skills do you do to give your mood a boost," most people don't have the answer. Or they say call a friend.

What if the phones are dead? That's depressing.

"Only boring people are bored. Just because you're not doing something, it doesn't mean that you're bored. You may have consciously chosen to do nothing, or what may look like "nothing" to others. Example: I'm making up my mind to sit here and watch two hours of soap operas, or to read. While you are doing that, try your best to not let your mind wander to things that are not right here in the moment with you.

"Loneliness impels lack of socialization and connection with other people. It's not about quantity, it's about quality. For people who are lonely, one of the best things they can do is find a volunteer position where they are working with other people, are giving back through the work and having faith the connections will start to happen. It's not going to happen sitting on your couch in your living room."

I asked Dr. Billiot if loneliness was a subject that comes up frequently in counseling.

She said 60 percent of the people who come to her complain of feeling lonely, which—not surprisingly—matched the number I heard on CBS. "Feeling lonely is a normal human feeling. Loneliness by itself is not the problem; it depends on how often and how long you feel lonely. Everybody feels lonely sometimes and feels like they are alone in the world. We wouldn't be human if we didn't have those feelings occasionally. That's when you tell yourself to get out of your pity party. We are all alone in our heads with us.

"How much or how long do you feel lonely is an important question. Even people who are psychologically well adjusted feel lonely sometimes or they wouldn't be human. The question is do you have the skills to deal with it. Talk to a friend. Getting through hard times is what brings people together.

"Does a relationship fix everything? Does it keep you from feeling lonely? Remember you are the common denominator. No matter where you go, there you are. You can have millions of people around and still feel lonely. Share with your family and friends the bad times as well as the good times. It doesn't change who you are. You are still there in your own head. That's a fact we have to live with."

Feeling lonely is a normal feeling. The question is, do you have the skills to know what to do when you feel that way?

"People are often unwilling to make themselves open or vulnerable to other people. They tend to be more private. They don't want to be judged, so they don't open up.

"Now, people can live a private secluded life and people don't know we are lonely. Ask for help. People are so afraid of being rejected that won't take a risk and tell people how they are feeling. It's okay if you are conscious of doing that. It might be a first step."

As I reviewed the insights from Dr. Billiot a few conclusions came to mind. Feeling lonely is a normal human trait we all share, but for many people it is severe enough to cause problems. For all of us, it is important to acknowledge loneliness and develop the skills to know what we need to do when we are feeling lonely. What works for you?

Judy W. Stamper LMHC on Depression and Age Group Differences
How Social Media Magnifies Loneliness in Our Youth

When I asked Judy Stamper what percentage of her patients complained of loneliness and or depression, she answered 70-80 percent.

I asked her if she found it to be age specific and she said not really. It is her view, based on the experience of over 25 years of private practice, that the world is changing.

Among the correlations that she mentioned is the isolation from human contact. Over the last five or ten years as our culture has changed and our media has changed and social devices have changed, we have become faster paced. Social media has become so prevalent that people have become more isolated.

The more disconnected you feel from friends, family, community, passions, hobbies and human contact, she explained, the lonelier your feel.

Anxiety, loneliness and depression can spin off into physiologic problems. If you don't have strong human connections it can make you physically sick, with headaches, stomach aches, and just general malaise afflicting the physical body. Because from a spiritual perspective, if we don't have strong human connection it's almost like there is a little part of us that kind of gets smaller.

DEPRESSION IN OUR YOUTH

Facebook, Twitter, Snapchat, Instagram are among the problems.

Social media affects each age group differently. During the developmental age of middle school to 18, our youth are extremely self-conscious about themselves, and if they get negative messages about themselves if makes them feel even worse. They feel they are under a microscope. Just the other day she saw another article in the paper about the high percentage of teenage suicides.

"They are so fragile, and kids can be anonymously mean. Social media can magnify the low self-esteem that leads to depression and even medication. Mean comments can be posted and can be devastating."

What's the answer?

She believes the key is that parents need to encourage and help their children find their interests and passions that they can carry through their life. They need to get their nose out of social media. Spark their passion and creativity to connect with their creator which will help them feel more health, happiness and a joyful life. "They can find ways to express their creative energy other than in social media. This is not to say social media is inherently harmful. It can be good in some ways, but should not become their whole life. This is true for adults as well as children."

She believes parents need to help their kids understand how it can affect them if they use it too much, and then let the kids decide how much to use it. Interestingly enough, research shows when given this choice the kids usually cut it down to between one and one and a half hours a day.

Judy shared with me that 30 to 40 percent of her practice consists of 15 to 25 year olds. And she loves this because they are hopeful, bright and enthusiastic. It's a niche that she loves. They are so salvageable, and she believes she can influence their lives when she helps them connect some dots and gives them unconditional support to find who they really are.

She said she has discovered that there is major anxiety among our youth. Forty percent feel a negative impact due to social media, and even more from divorce. Others suffer from early expectations. People are working hard in our society to get ahead. Children three, four and five years old are using an iPad and then we expect them to sit in a classroom and be still.

I asked her what would you say to a patient who comes in and says, I feel lonely, I feel depressed? Aside from medication, that is ...

The key is to find your passion and creativity. Check out the library. Just browse and see what draws you in. Maybe poetry will inspire you. Maybe there is a talk of film coming up, or a concert.

She shared an example of a patient who joined a pool league, as in shooting pool, not swimming in a pool. He honed his skills as a pool player and found his passion there. Check out different churches to see if you can connect with people. In Greek the word church means "people." But it doesn't have to be organized religion. There are free meditation groups meeting in most areas, some with spiritual affiliations, others secular. The point is that connections and passions often rise together.

"It" can be anything that gets you out in the world to connect with people who have the same interest.

Texting for an appointment for a phone conversation

Judy touched on the impersonal nature of contact—or lack of contact—with texting instead of picking up the phone and talking with someone. She said it's no secret the younger generation would rather text. Her son and daughter would rather text. So, she'll text them and ask if they can give her call when they have a chance. Texting to make an appointment to talk on the phone—I get it, I do the same thing with my son.

Are you connected with yourself?

Judy said that often the biggest disconnection to be faced In overcoming loneliness is the disconnection within yourself. What do you do spiritually? Do you have a practice? What are your thoughts? What do you do to feed you mind? What do you do to exercise? Come up with a few sentences as affirmations or positives phrases that you can say inwardly to start a shift to change your thoughts. You must start with yourself.

People who have a deep faith, no matter what it is, tend to get healthier faster—mentally, physically and spiritually. Faith in a source greater than yourself is a way to affirm that you are not alone.

Connect to gratitude – How do we love ourself?

What are the things we tell ourself every day? Move into gratitude and away from what is lacking. Gratitude is like a little seed in your heart that you plant and watch it grow. Gratitude fertilizes your heart.

Connecting to gratitude opens your internal joy. At the core of all the issues and problems is the question, how do we love ourselves.

What are the things we tell ourself every day? If we talk about how lonely we are, ask what we have that we might be grateful for rather than what we are lacking? Plant that little seed that fertilizes your heart.

Focus on what you are grateful for rather than what you are lacking. It really does all come down to learning to love oneself.

Shy People Are Forced to Find a Strategy
Become an "Expert" on Something and People will Come to You

We might think of shy people as fighting a life-long battle against loneliness, but in some ways, they may be the lucky ones. Knowing they are shy may have forced them to find long-term accommodations, whereas the formerly gregarious person who through life's circumstances finds him or herself feeling suddenly alone might feel adrift on uncharted seas.

When I was talking with a friend about my book one evening, she told me that when she was younger, she was very shy, which surprised me. I never got that impression from her. She said she read a book when she was sixteen about how to overcome being shy.

Since I had always been an extravert this concept had never occurred to me. She said the idea in the book was to pick a career that you could become an expert or authority in and people would have to come to you for information, help or advice. This way you didn't have to go out and seek a connection with people. They would come to you.

This concept led her down the path to coming a successful and well thought of CPA. In addition to being very skilled professionally, she has endeared herself and become a good friend and confidant to many of her clients over the years. She is a warm-hearted, caring person who has found her path to developing connections and life-long friends.

Section Five

THE MANY PATHS TO CONNECTION:
AS VARIED AS LIFE'S ADVENTURES

Some of the following chapters describe the experiences of the author, while others are derived from interviews with people facing the same challenges. What path will help you feed your soul? How do you find it? The first step in finding your path is to seek it.

A Journey Of Healing, My Story of Reconnecting And Feeding My Soul—

The Loss Of A Spouse Or Loved One Can Be The Ultimate Test

Just about the time you think life is running great and you have everything under control, everything changes. The lesson, it seems, is that we should always expect to face the unexpected—for better or for worse. Apparently, having everything "under control" is just an illusion.

After three surgeries, one round of chemotherapy and radiation, my husband Tony and I lost the battle. His cancer metastasized. We fought it as hard and as long as we possibly could, with the help of all the medical experts and prayers that we could solicit, but the diagnosis was not a good one to begin with. Small bowel cancer is so rare that there has not been enough research done on it to have developed an effective treatment.

I learned that cancers that are more mainstream, such as breast cancer and colon cancer tend to get more funding for research and treatment development. I suppose this makes sense, but logic is seldom of any comfort when we find ourselves being swept downstream through life's rapids.

The doctors gave him the same chemo cocktail that they give colon cancer patients, which we were told was the best they had to offer. It was certainly not a sure thing by a long shot, but it never is—even when it's one of the more common cancers. Even after going through the side effects of chemo, there was no guarantee, but our oncologist told us that if it was his father, he would recommend going through this chemo protocol. That was all we needed to hear. It was good enough for us. But really, what choice did we have? There are times in life when, as hard as it might be, we are forced to give up our natural desire to be in control, and hand it over to the doctors, or maybe to God. This can be a very hard lesson to learn.

Even with the limited knowledge of this strain of cancer, believe me when I say we did everything we could to fight it. The survival rate after five years is only five percent. Of course, we believed with all of our heart that we were going to be in that five percent.

It was during this time that I began my first book, *An Astrologer's Journey*. In January of 2011 Tony had just been diagnosed with cancer. Surgery was scheduled within days of the diagnosis because it is such an aggressive cancer. Surgery was followed by chemotherapy, beginning six weeks later. I choose to take the time while he was recovering and undergoing treatment to immerse myself in writing my book. It had been my dream and goal for many years, and I finally found the discipline to do it. I was feeling it, but it was also written in the stars.

I knew that Saturn, the planet that is the

disciplinarian, the tester and the teacher was making his journey through my 3rd house, indicating a cycle of mental structure and discipline. When Saturn is traveling through this area of a person's chart it is important to be mentally structured and focused. And what better way to harness that energy then to tackle writing my first book.

I knew that my outside activities would be limited because I would be staying close to home during his treatment, so I felt it would be good therapy for me and for him. Writing kept me upbeat and in a positive frame of mind. I learned by doing it that writing was nurturing to my soul. Saturn, the teacher was serving me well. He was keeping me focused and working at home with a positive attitude as we were going through treatment for this rare and horrible disease.

> **Life is never the same after losing a spouse, even when you are prepared and think that you are ready.**

I have always kept a journal since I was a little girl, but never did I write with the intention of anyone reading it. In fact, I plan to burn all of my journals before I die—if I get the chance anyway. I'm not sure exactly what day that will be, but here's hoping it will be many years in the future!

The writing of my first published book was different from writing my journals. It was written with the intent of sharing a story and information that I hoped would be motivational and helpful—and it was, for many people.

But I've written this book to "feed MY soul." If it also feeds your soul, that's a blessing.

My background is certainly very eclectic and

diverse which is probably why I was motivated to share my struggles and adventures. But when my husband first passed away in June of 2015, I wasn't ready to openly write or even talk about it. I'm sure others who have suffered loss have experienced something similar. I wanted to, but I just couldn't bring myself to sit down at my computer and open my heart. It was too painful.

I remember reading a book a friend loaned to me soon after Tony's death called *Magical Thinking* by Joan Didion. Her husband had a fatal heart attack at the dinner table. Although she was already a renowned author, she wrote in her book that she was unable to write again for two years after her husband died. At the time I thought that was odd. Why two years? My husband had just passed away and I was still in a fog, but I didn't know it.

I thought I was doing just fine. He had been declining for a couple of years and I thought I was ready to heal and go on. Again, just as the cancer and its treatment had been beyond my control, so was the timing of my recovery. *I learned that it takes as long as it takes to heal . . . to find yourself again, or to reinvent yourself.*

Transiting Jupiter in the 3rd house

Then a little over a year after Tony passed, I was, of course, following my astrology chart and saw that Jupiter, the guardian angel and benefic, was about to begin her one-year journey through my third house of communication. I knew that if I was ever going to write another book, this would be the time. It was now or never. It was the right time to begin writing and sharing my healing journey—my journey of reinventing and rediscovering myself.

And once I had begun the writing became a big part of the healing process.

To me, writing a book is like the old adage about eating an elephant—the only way to do it is one bite at a time. And once you start, the ideas and energy flow. It all comes together. I'd wake up at 4:30 in the morning with ideas and a need to write about the thoughts that are running through my head. So I've learned to keep a note pad next to my bed, and since I sleep alone I can turn the light on and write them down. Then eventually, I just started getting up at 5 a.m. and going to my computer.

Jupiter Retrograde Extends Opportunity

Fortunately, I knew that Jupiter was going to be going retrograde while it was traveling through my 3rd house of communications, which would extent her beneficial influence on my motivation to write. I knew I needed to take advantage of this cycle, and I could see by what was flowing out of me that the time had come to "get it down on paper." My healing journey had begun, but it wasn't an easy journey and for the first time in my life I truly understood the old saying, "two steps forward, one step back."

Life is never the same after losing a spouse, even when you are prepared and think that you are ready. Four years and seven months after my husband was diagnosed with small bowel cancer, after three surgeries and one round of chemo and a round of radiation treatment, it finally took over his body.

I guess I can be grateful for the three good years we had before the cancer metastasized. I'm certainly grateful for the fifteen wonderful years we shared together before his diagnosis. But it was difficult to keep sight of that as the pet scans where showing the fatal diagnosis.

Although I had already lost one husband to heart disease, it did not make losing Tony any easier. As I look back, I do feel blessed to have had two very special, wonderful men in my life, knowing many women never find one.

Both of my deceased husbands were very special men. They will be in my heart forever. I can close my eyes and see them, healthy and happy, sharing a laugh or lifting a glass of wine with me. And I remember the role each of them played in making me the woman I am today.

Although they were both Sagittarians, they were very different in their personalities. Larry had an 11th house sun, which tends to be a more social and outgoing personality. He loved a good party, enjoyed his friends, was a very active member of Rotary and enjoyed his MG car club friends. He was always ready to entertain.

Tony had a 12th house sun, which was an indication to me as an astrologer that he enjoyed his alone time, his solitude. Although he was charming and interactive in his profession, all he really wanted or needed was to be with me after he retired. I guess that is why it was so different after he passed. We pretty much did everything together, especially during his last few years with me. We traveled; we watched golf, tennis, football, and the Olympics on TV, and often went out to lunch or dinner. We enjoyed our time together. It was easy. It was comfortable. It was a great life until that nasty cancer reared its ugly head in his body.

At first it seemed so unfair. Why him? He had never really been sick a day from the time when I met him. He had good genes. Tony's father was in his late eighties when we first met. Tony was very active and healthy. He jogged, played golf, and worked out on his Boflex. This was very important to me, since my previous husband passed away at fifty-eight and his father also passed away at fifty-eight with a heart attack.

His mother had passed away with breast cancer when she was in her 50s, but we were told that breast cancer and small bowel are totally unrelated. Her cancer had not predisposed him to this. Of course, we never in our wildest imagination ever dreamed that he would get the Big "C" of any variety. Does anyone ever think about getting cancer? I know we didn't. I guess if you have a genetic predisposition that's one thing, and somehow easier to accept? Probably not. But who ever heard of getting small bowel cancer—whoever even heard of it at all?

This year, an estimated 10,190 adults (5,380 men and 4,810 women) in the United States will be diagnosed with small bowel cancer. It is estimated that 1,390 deaths (770 men and 620 women) from this disease will occur this year.

For comparison, colorectal cancer, the third most common cancer in both men and women in the United States, will be diagnosed 13 times as often. This year, an estimated 135,430 adults in the United States will be diagnosed with colorectal cancer. (*statistics, cancer.net*)

So, we were both shocked when he was diagnosed. As I noted earlier, our oncologist told us that there was no proven protocol treatment for it, since it was so rare. But they had been using a similar chemo formula that was used for colon cancer patients. The survival statistics were against us, even with chemo, and we knew the chemo was going to make him so sick. We were hesitant. But our oncologist told us that if it were him or his family member, he would encourage having the chemo.

The first step was surgery, and after a nasty, major surgery to remove the growing tumors, the surgeon declared he got it all. This was followed by a precautionary six months of chemo. Our lives changed dramatically during this time. He slowed down, lost a lot of weight, and I chose this time to begin my first book while taking care of him.

I lost my job

When he passed there was such a huge void in my life. I felt like I had lost my job. My job for the previous five years—the five years since his cancer was first diagnosed—was to take care of him. We had three good years in that time before the cancer came roaring back, and for that I'm thankful. But even then I was focused on Tony.

Changes In Latitude, Changes In Attitude
Healing is a Journey and Travel Can Help

Travel is always a good distraction or antidote to help in the healing process—or at least I thought it would be after my husband's death. My first trip was to San Diego to visit my aunt and uncle about six months after Tony passed away. I did the very same thing when Larry passed away.

Traveling, getting away, escaping—"changes in latitude, changes in attitude," as the Jimmy Buffett song goes—was my first instinct. But unfortunately, no matter where you go, there you are. I couldn't run away from the feeling of loss deep in the pit of my stomach. The memories and heartbreak followed me no matter where I was.

He was always in my DNA, always in the back of my mind and my memory bank. There was that feeling of being disconnected. I remember on my first trip after he passed, I really missed calling him first thing in the morning as I had when I woke up on previous trips to California before his death. I'd wake up at 5 or 6 a.m. when it was 8 or 9 a.m. in Florida. I'd usually catch him as he was on his way to the golf course.

Tony did enjoy his time to himself and didn't mind if I was away on a speaking engagement or visiting family. But he was always happy to hear my voice when I called, just as I was happy to hear his.

Tony was born with his sun in the 12th house. People who have their sun in the 12th house in their astrological chart tend to enjoy their solitary time. I think that was one of the reasons we got along so well right from the very beginning. I gave him the space and time that he needed for himself. And my 9th house sun loved and needed space and freedom and independence. I loved to travel and so did he, so we had a good balance of time together and apart.

We certainly did our share of traveling before his diagnosis. But after that we were always afraid to plan anything too far in advance. We never knew when that PET scan was going to bring us bad news, as it eventually did.

I'll never forget the day I found out "it" was back. He had gone in for one of his routine follow-up appointments with his oncologist while I was away. My son had taken my grandson and me on a cruise for my birthday. Tony was not a cruiser. Even ferry boats made him seasick. This cruise was just a long weekend to Mexico—a bonding time for my son, grandson and me. It was a beautiful opportunity and I was smiling inside.

I did try to get Tony to reschedule his oncology appointment until after my return. I had been to every single one of his oncologist appointments with him. They were always fine when I was there. No change until this one, like it had somehow snuck through in my absence.

I was driving home from the cruise when I called home and he gave me the bad news. He said the PET scan showed spots. I felt like someone had hit me in the stomach and knocked all the wind out of my lungs.

At that time we didn't even know the extent of what "spots" really meant, or just how bad it was. It was when I went with him to his next appointment that we learned that the cancer had metastasized. There were several spots—as the doctor called them—and when he mentioned the liver and lungs I knew it was not good. Little did we know that that Tony would be gone in less than two years.

Fortunately we did enjoy our life—the many things we did together including traveling—prior to cancer hitting us. I say *us* because it was a major life change for both of us.

Everyone loses or has lost someone at one time or another in their life. It would be impossible to go through this life without experiencing that pain—the pain of the loss of a loved one or a friend. Some of us have felt that pain many more times than others. It seems that no matter how many times we experience it, the hurt and healing is something that we have to go through. Unfortunately it is a very personal process. No one can do it for us. No one can carry the cross. No one can cry our tears. No one can stop the heartaches. No one can convince you that the sun always rises until at long last you see it inching above the horizon. And no one can make the pain go away any faster than the healing of time will allow. Healing is a journey. It is a sad, lonely journey that we each process and deal with in our own private special way.

Everyone deals with loss in their own way and

in their own time ... and among the many things that makes each of us different, I have learned that each sun sign has their own way of dealing with their loss, which I will talk about later.

In true Aries fashion, and with the help of my wonderful Virgo sister, within a week of his passing I had all of the furniture removed from his office, which is where the hospital bed had been. I had the room painted and went out and bought a very comfortable queen size bed. I have turned his office into an official guest room which is something we never had before—his office had a sofa bed which doubled as a guest room. My grandson is thoroughly enjoying the new bed. And I so enjoy his visits.

From Purpose to New Purpose

I believe that the magnitude and duration of the healing process depends a great deal on the role we had in the daily life of the person who passed on. For example, in my case I was my husband's caregiver for the months leading up to his passing. He filled the major part of my life and my daily routine. He was my foremost purpose and in the forefront on my mind at all times.

When he finally lost his battle with small bowel cancer I felt I had lost my purpose in life. My purpose was to take care of him—take him to his doctor's appointments, prepare his meals, keep him company. We watched all the golf tournaments and tennis matches together. He especially loved the major golf tournaments. Before his cancer started getting the best of him, he enjoyed playing golf a couple times each week. In fact, he was the reason I learned to play. It wasn't too long after we started dating that I decided that it would probably be a good idea if I learned to play. And as it turned out, it was a great idea.

We enjoyed many wonderful golfing vacations together. He especially loved playing the courses in Scottsdale, Arizona. Although the summers are brutally hot, we would stay on our Eastern Time Zone schedule and get up 4 a.m. for a 6 a.m. tee time. We watched many sunrises over the desert.

Memories . . . they are wonderful and I'm told they are part of the healing process. Yes, it is a process. Wouldn't it be wonderful if you could just open a can of "heal yourself" and all of the pain and sorrow would be gone, sort of a "pain no more" remedy?

But we all know that just isn't the way it works. It's a slow journey, and I the amount of time that it takes depends not only on your closeness in the last days, weeks, months or years, but also on the depth of your relationship before the illness. I know that my husband's adult daughters, who live out of town, spoke with him every day on the phone. So he was a daily part of their life, even if just for thirty minutes. His sister talked with him every day over the phone about the stock market. She said that when he left she lost her enthusiasm and interest in the market. It just wasn't the without him.

It's said that the loss of a spouse or child is one of the most difficult things that you can go through. I tend to agree with that to a certain point, but having also lost both of my parents I can still recall the pain and deep sense of loss. I guess we expect that our parents are going to die before us, but we don't think of our spouse or children ever dying—unless of course they are diagnosed with cancer. Then we live with that fear looming over our head every day. We dig deep into our emotional reservoir and learn the meaning of the saying, "Make the most of every day."

As I approached the one-year mark after his passing, those life memories of *us* began to find their way back into my consciousness. Most of them were beautiful, but the sad final days were there as well. In either case it seemed as if Tony was there, again holding my hand, giving me faith and courage to take the next step, and to enjoy each new sunrise. Watching the sun rise over the Atlantic in those early dark days built my confidence and continues to do so today.

> *"You won't die in the middle of the night if you've got something in the morning that you've got to do."* — Carl Ryner

Life Is Always Evolving

Try To Enjoy The Ride!

In my first book I discussed the path I followed to astrology. It was a path with many stops along the way, including meditation and traditional religion. Always, the search was for a way to get in touch with myself and understand why I felt the way I did, and how I fit into the order of the universe. Astrology gave me a way of *seeing* that made the most sense to me. First off, I learned that by following the lunar cycle I could better understand and appreciate my emotions and the cycles of my emotions.

When my love and interest in astrology began back in the early 1980s, I was single and looking for my prince charming. This was during the era when Linda Goodman's sun sign book had just come out and Nancy Reagan's use of astrology became public knowledge. Yes, for those of you who don't remember or were not yet born, it was quite a big deal when it first was revealed that Nancy Reagan was consulting with an astrologer to help President Ronald Reagan.

Timing is everything and astrology can be a valuable tool to help select the best time to achieve the best results, so I assumed she consulted her astrologer to help him with timing for scheduling his various meetings so that he would get the best possible results.

I was delighted when I had the opportunity to attend one of Linda Goodman's astrology talks at a major conference back in the 80s when I was a student of astrology—not that we ever stop learning, but I was a novice back then.

> **After a long and tedious journey, I was reeling with emotions and trying to find my new normal.**

My personal interest and studies began as a hobby and developed into a career. Along the way, I was blessed and fortunate that I did meet two "prince charmings." Although I lost both of them, after I was left alone I felt very fortunate that I had an interest and a career that I was passionate about.

When Tony and I first moved to the beach in 2012, after he retired, I sort of put my career on the back burner. I cut back on my consultation appointments and did not really connect professionally with our new community. I was more involved and focused on decorating our new home, entertaining our families, and traveling.

Life was good. He was my prince and I was his princess. We enjoyed our new home and our new retired life. And he, at that time, was in perfect health. He exercised regularly, ate a healthy diet, never smoked and only drank wine occasionally. He had a great attitude about life. He always saw the glass half full rather than half empty. He was the epitome of a Sagittarian. He was my soul mate and we led a charmed life together.

So when he was diagnosed in November of 2010 with the cancer that would later take his life, you could have knocked me over with a feather. I was devastated to say the least. I have already spoken of how this changed my life and his, keeping us closer to home than we had become accustomed to as the happy travelers.

So with this new challenge came an opportunity—a chance to write the book I'd been thinking about for so long. This time while I was taking care of him would be my time to write, and to feed my soul. Writing became my window to the world, my haven, my motivation. Life was still good because he was still there with me. He had a great attitude and spirit even when he was recovering from his surgery and going through chemo. And I was happy to be there, writing *An Astrologer's Journey, My Life With the Stars* and taking care of my husband.

My first book was published in November of 2011, one year after his diagnosis. I was so happy that he was able to come to my first book signing. We continued to live a relatively normal life after he completed his treatment. By that time frequent and regular follow-up tests and visits with his oncologist had come to feel normal. Then, three years into his remission, the devastating blow struck us. His cancer had metastasized. There were spots on his liver, small bowel, and lung. This was not good.

Another surgery was scheduled, followed by

radiation for the spot on his lung. Unfortunately, this was the beginning of the end for us. I was once again going to lose my prince charming.

Coming out of the closet with astrology

After a long and tedious journey, I was reeling with emotions and trying to find my new normal. Yes, there is still a period of shock and disbelief even when you know the end is inevitable. Even though I knew it was coming and could see the handwriting on the wall, it still didn't make it any easier. So when he was gone I did the only thing I knew how to do—I threw myself back into my work and "came out of the closet" in my local community.

I started scheduling local workshops and talks. I joined the local Chamber of Commerce. I not only joined, but I became very active and involved. I joined a networking leads group that met once a week. And I went to all the ribbon cuttings and after hours social events. Now granted, this would not be a healing therapy for everyone, but it seemed to work for me.

Maybe it was the answer to my prayers. I can remember sitting out by the pool one day at my son's house, not too long after Tony passed away, watching the sunrise shimmering through the trees. It made me think of God and feel his presence. I started speaking to God.

"Help me find my path and direction as I travel through this new journey. Help me to be clear minded and to be a better person and know that You are always with me. I am never alone. I feel Your presence as I am looking through the trees at the sunrise."

I actually wrote this in my journey that morning which is why I remembered it so clearly.

Yes, I kept a journal which is one of the things that is strongly recommended when dealing with a loss. It's a wonderful way to process your feelings and move through the healing journey.

Introduction to BAUD therapy

It wasn't long after my conversation with God that the psychologist I was seeing for grief counseling introduced me to a treatment called BAUD, which is a Bio Acoustical Utilization Device. This is a relatively new neurological treatment that is used for "reset therapy." My therapist's father, Dr. George Lindenfeld, was instrumental in researching and developing this technique.

This treatment is very cutting edge and involves sound waves and using a headset. I must admit that I was a little leery of being a part of something that was so newly developed without much of a track record in the field. But at the same time it was also an exciting idea to be part of a new therapy. And since I am an adventurous, pioneering Aries, I thought *why not*? I was suffering from so much pain and depression that I was willing to try anything that might help speed up the healing process. Besides, Aries are always eager to do things fast. For me, going through the healing and grieving process needed to be accelerated.

Fast doesn't always mean easy. It was very emotionally draining and painful in the beginning, but I could see that progress was being made as the treatments continued. In the beginning I cried even more that I had in the days and weeks after his death. But there in-between the tears was a feeling of peace and serenity. I stayed with this treatment for several weeks, and when that time was up I knew I had made progress on my journey. Yes it was fast, which was exactly what I was looking for and needed.

Dr. Lindenfeld is very passionate about getting the information about this treatment out to the public but only under the right circumstances. My therapist feels strongly that BAUD therapy should only be approached under the supervision and guidance of a professional who is trained and certified in the technique. For more information, you can check out this website. BAUD is a Powerful Therapy Tool. http://baudtherapy.com/studies.html

The treatment helped me through the recovery period when I couldn't stop crying. I'd wake up crying and I'd fall asleep crying. I was fortunate to find an excellent psychologist in my hometown who was trained in this treatment, considering that there are only 210 trained BAUD therapists in the entire country.

I believe the treatment saved me months of extended crying and depression. Not that grieving and depression aren't normal or necessary after experiencing a loss, I just found this treatment to be a great aid and tool to help me to process my emotions. It was a tremendous release mechanism. As painful as it was in the beginning, it was well worth the time and energy it took.

I don't know how I would have felt had I not gone through the treatment or what my time frame would have been to return to a "normal" life without crying every day, but I believe it was an invaluable tool to help me through the healing journey. Maybe I would have discovered another therapy that would have helped, but I do know this: recovery is only possible if you participate in the process.

That might require taking chances, taking a leap of faith and trusting the net will appear if you need it. You can't sit back and wait for the new you to emerge like a butterfly from a cocoon. You might well continue to live some kind of a life safe inside your cocoon; you might even see the sun rise every day, but you might never again fully appreciate it.

Creating a day worth living:
Get up early, express gratitude for what you have. Do something productive. Do something fun. Do something for someone else.
— cornercanyoncounseling.com

Connect With Others
By Connecting With Yourself
Don't Be Surprised By Your Own Resistance

In an effort to find myself after my husband passed away, I decided to take a one year anniversary trip. I indulged myself in what would turn out to be a life changing experience. It came about very accidentally.

It all began in April of 2016 when Krista, my very dear friend and yoga teacher, invited me to a Qigong Healing Forum presented by teacher Jeff Primack in Daytona Beach. I had never heard of Qigong, but since it was close to home and I could sleep in my own bed every night, I decided to check it out. I have always respected and appreciated Krista's judgment. She knew I was going through an adjustment and grieving process after the loss of my husband and felt it might be something that would be helpful to me.

So I did a little research and learned Qigong has roots in Chinese medicine, philosophy, and martial arts. And is traditionally viewed as a practice to cultivate and balance chi, translated as "life energy."

This certainly piqued my interest—enough for me to register for the weekend forum. And believe me when I say that I was not disappointed. The forum ranged wide and deep into how we can best balance our life energy. It was not only about physical and mental exercise, it also covered nutrition, healthy eating, and the importance of breathing. We learned about red pepper paste and smoothies, and I'll share those recipes with you later.

Finding a new Spiritual connection in Hawaii

Throughout the weekend I felt sure I was taking on good fuel for my healing journey. I was moving forward, and had the weekend been the end of it, I would have felt satisfied. However, as if on cue, I learned that Jeff was offering a seven-day Qigong retreat in Hawaii in June. Luck, or divine providence, continued to shape the moment when I realized I was already planning a trip to California to visit my aunt in San Diego the week before the retreat was to begin. It was a like a bolt of lightning hit me when I realized the synchronicity of this retreat with my already scheduled trip to California. So I meditated during the weekend of the Daytona Beach forum about registering for the retreat in Hawaii. I am at heart a practical person—which is perhaps why I chose astrology as a path—but it certainly felt like this was divine providence, like something I was destined to do. And after all, I kept reminding myself, I would already be half way to Hawaii when I was in California.

When I studied my astrology chart for the dates of the Hawaii retreat, I saw that all of the stars were aligned and it was exactly what I needed to do. I felt that this trip would be a major part of my "healing journey" and I would return home different, more evolved, with a mended soul.

* * *

I was still feeling the amazing impact the conference in Daytona Beach had on my life, so I could only imagine what a week at a retreat in Hawaii would do for me—and at this moment *me* had to be my focus. I was still practicing as an astrologer and helping other people with the challenges in their lives while I was healing and adjusting to the loss of my husband. I felt that I needed to take this opportunity to work solely on myself and regain my inner peace and strength. Yes, my expectations were very high after the growth I experienced in one weekend. Now bear in mind that I did not know a single soul who was planning to attend this retreat, except for Jeff, the instructor, but that fact didn't frighten me. I was being drawn to Hawaii almost thoughtlessly, like sailors drawn in by the song of a sea nymph. I knew instinctively that the call I was hearing was genuine. And believe me when I say that I was not disappointed.

With all the pieces synchronizing naturally, the decision to go to Hawaii was simple. All I had to do was say yes. The siren song of the big island of Hawaii was calling, but there was one more factor:

the retreat, just a few months off now, was in June—the one-year anniversary of my husband's passing. I have a beautiful condo on the ocean, but I had no desire to be there at that this time.

I was planning to fly home from California the exact same day the retreat was to begin, so still feeling a Qigong afterglow, I moved quickly and changed my travel plans.

It was Monday June 27th, 2016. I was so excited; I couldn't believe the day had actually come. Still, as the dream was finally unfolding, I suddenly experienced mixed emotions about this adventure. Although I had lived on Oahu in my youth when my father was stationed in the Navy, I had never been to the Big Island of Hawaii. This was going to be a totally new territory and experience for me.

My fears were soon overcome by the joy and optimism I felt as the last few days ticked away. I wanted to soar and enjoy each experience of this "retreat." For those who are interested in astrology, you would appreciate everything that was going on in my chart the day I arrived on the Island. For others, let's just say all my ducks were lining up— that is, very supportive astrologically speaking. You might not be surprised to hear I actually studied my chart for this trip before I made the commitment. I knew from what I saw this would be an exciting, life changing experience—the trip of a lifetime. I had believed that from the moment I first heard about it. I was excited and ready for the unknown adventure, but I had to know what my chart said.

I had read Elizabeth Gilbert's book *Eat, Pray, Love*. I even saw the movie, several times, which totally captured my emotions. So when I embarked on this Hawaiian Retreat adventure I was excited. I wasn't expecting to find the "love" part of the book, but I did have very strong Jupiter/Mars connections going on, which could indicate a romantic connection. At the very least it was going to be a wonderful adventure, which is what it turned out to be. So as it turned out, for my one year anniversary of Tony's passing I had chosen to begin with pray, not eat or love, which is why I chose this Qigong retreat.

I was in very good spirits as I embarked for the San Diego airport on what I felt certain would be a spiritual journey. I knew in my heart this was going to be an amazing week. It was going to help me rediscover the light within me so I could appreciate and honor it. I felt fortunate and blessed to be able to do this at this time in my life. I began to feel the serenity and calmness as I started to do the Qigong breathing exercises as a part of my daily routine. What I didn't know was how much hard work it was going to be.

The first day. Upon arriving on the Big Island, I was overwhelmed by its beauty. I didn't realize it was an agricultural island. The retreat compound where I stayed was on the Kona side of the island, also known as the rainy side. We were very fortunate that it mostly rained only at night during our retreat.

When I landed at the little Kona airport, I felt like I had entered another word or dimension in time. Jeff Primack, the Qigong instructor, was also our chauffeur and tour guide and made our first introductions to what appeared to be a very unpopulated and beautiful emerald in the middle of the Pacific.

This was certainly very different from when I had lived in Hawaii as a child with my family when my father was in the Navy stationed on Oahu. We had lived on Waikiki, which even at that time was much more populated than the Big Island. This was totally new territory and a new experience for me.

The drive up the mountain to the compound was amazingly beautiful. I had absolutely no comprehension of the beauty and experiences that I was going to encounter over the next week. I knew there would be no electricity and that "the facilities" were the outdoor variety. It was sort of like camping with running water.

There was no air conditioning, but there always seemed to be a nice island breeze and it rained a part of every day, so I never felt hot. In fact, it was actually cool in the evenings when the sun went down. The outdoor shower stalls had running hot and cold water and were located across a field about 100 yards from my cabin. Right next to them were two community sinks for brushing your teeth and washing your hands. The outdoor flushing toilet stalls were about 100 yards in the opposite direction. So I got lots of exercise. And even though I didn't need to, I did lose weight.

The modest, sparsely furnished two-person cabins had very comfortable posturepedic mattresses. I slept like a baby every night. The open-air screening allowed the tropical breeze to cool the evening air.

There are no words to describe the quiet and isolated feeling of this compound. It was surrounded by natural running streams and beautiful waterfalls. It was like nothing I had ever seen or experienced before. I felt like I was in a movie. I felt surrounded by God and angels. But it was a huge adjustment. I did not have a roommate. No electricity, no computer, no cell phone, no TV, no internet and NO WINE. What was a person to do?

I will confess that for a moment when I first arrived and saw the facilities I wanted to run, to fly back to civilization in California, but instead I focused on centering myself, on seeing the upside to being free from our devises. This was truly going to be a spiritual, healing time with no distractions. It was as close to connecting with nature as I had ever been. The evening sky was like a field of diamonds with no electric lights or emissions to mask its beauty. The moon was in the last quarter of its waning phase, so there was not much in the way of light of the moon to compete with the dark of the night.

It was truly a paradise retreat with the exception of the deep emotional work that lay ahead of me.

We were told during our orientation meeting that coffee and papaya would be available in the dome, which was a picturesque walk across a green field. The kitchen was also there with a generator that provided the only electricity in the compound. The outdoor bathroom facility, which did flush, was on the way. Our morning breathing and Qigong practice would begin at 8 a.m. in an outdoor covered pavilion overlooking a spectacular running stream which fed into a waterfall. This was truly God's country. There is no other way to describe it.

We met the staff and our fellow journeyers during this first gathering in the dome. I was very surprised to learn that all of the participants had traveled to Hawaii from Florida. Here I was 5,000 miles from home meeting people who lived only 60 miles from me.

After coffee and papaya, we walked to the open air pavilion overlooking the mountain stream and got right to work. Jeff led us into a Qigong breathing exercise. It was so powerful and intense that it brought out an overflow of emotions in me. Unspoken prayer was pouring out of my heart. It was intense to say the least. At that moment I knew my life-changing quest had begun in earnest.

It wasn't all smooth and easy. It took me several days to decompress and recompose from the high drive, high gear activities that I was used to in my daily life. After my husband passed away the previous year I went into overdrive. In my true Arian nature, my survival mode was to stay busy. Every sun sign has its way of coping and that was mine. So this retreat was totally a foreign path for me. No connection to the outside world. Was this to become my new reality? Really? Would I be able to achieve and maintain a sense of peace and acceptance within myself without exterior distractions and stimulations? I gave myself over, allowing the retreat's benefits in, rather than resisting them.

In addition to the physical and mental healing benefits of this retreat, I learned a great deal about the benefits our instructor Jeff Primack describes in his book, *Food—Healing Cooking with Qi.*

Each morning when we first got up we were offered a variation of a fresh healthy smoothie, or half of a papaya, and coffee or tea. After our Qigong practice which usually took anywhere between an hour or two we enjoyed our choice of a healthy omelet with a variation of fresh vegetables and/or goat cheese. Asparagus was my favorite and of course the home-made pepper paste which I have continued to make and share with my friends and neighbors. Some mornings we even had little fresh langostinos also known as baby lobsters that Jeff had caught in his mountain stream traps. I knew I wouldn't recall every delicious meal and desert, so I purchased Jeff's cookbook, and his smoothie book, *Smoothie Formulas*, which includes 95 delicious high-photochemical recipes.

My morning smoothie became a major part of my healing journey when I returned home. I have continued to enjoy making the "Anti-Inflammation Smoothie" for pain and arthritis.

RECIPE FOR "ANTI-INFLAMMATION SMOOTHIE"

2 c. distilled water

30 cherries, remove pits

½ organic cucumber

3 wedges papaya, no seeds.

1 inch ginger root

1 inch turmeric root

1 inch thick pineapple ring

1 pineapple stem

I tend to use a little more ginger and turmeric root then the recipe calls for and fewer cherries. I make this in a NutriBullet and divide it into two portions. I believe this has helped my arthritis and improved my energy level, and it's wonderful for the digestive system.

After a healthy, delicious breakfast Jeff would lead us on a spectacular hike or walk through the lush, tropical wooded fields covered with moss and ferns. Those who were more adventurous and sure-footed also explored the rock embedded streams where the water was constantly flowing.

I personally found it more within my comfort zone to stay on dry ground where I felt more secure. I certainly did not want to be evacuated back to the mainland in an air ambulance. I knew my limitations and I wasn't there to prove anything. I was there to find myself and redefine myself.

Going within to find peace and happiness

As I was coming to the end of this week of hard work, isolation, meditation, and transformation, I started thinking about how I was going to integrate this feeling of peacefulness into my daily life. I came to the conclusion that only I could make myself happy. I needed to internalize the experience and make it part of my biology, so I could go within naturally and without conscious manipulation to find peace and my personal happiness.

As the week wound down, I kept reminding myself that I was fortunate and blessed to have been able to make this journey. I wanted to savor every minute and enjoy the beauty of the tropical, mystical paradise. And I wanted to take home with me everything I had learned, everything I was feeling.

What changes did the Qigong retreat help create in me?

More energy and mental clarity

Better balance

Better focus and concentration

A feeling of calmness
More patience
Better nutrition and food education

I discovered that stress makes you tired. I was amazed that I wasn't ever really tired the entire time that I was there.

And as an added bonus, it even helped my golf game when I got back home by slowing down my backswing!

In fact, my new practice of Qigong helped open many doors for me. I grew healthier in body, mind, and spirit. It was an education in nutrition. It improved my physical movement and exercise practice. It gave me more energy as I learned breathing exercises to reach a deeper meditative state.

There were physiological benefits like improving my blood circulation, lowering my blood pressure, and the removal of dioxins from my body.

When I returned from Hawaii, I knew I was ready to begin on my second book. I had found the inner peace I needed. I now could look inside without as much fear. Sure it was difficult, but I no longer shied away from the reality.

Writing feeds my Soul . . .

I have learned over the years that writing feeds my soul and after my week in Hawaii my soul was in a feeding frenzy—calm but energized. Writing my daily posts on my *AstrologyTalk* Facebook page, my monthly Astrology Newsletter, my journal all feed my soul. The challenge, I told myself, was to find or make time to write another book.

I guess it wasn't until I really got motivated and felt that I had something to share again, something to say that could help others through their healing journey, that I made the commitment to myself to focus on this book. My one-year anniversary trip helped take me to that place.

What drives your engine? What are you passionate about? What motivates you to get out of bed and get moving in the morning? These are all thought provoking subjects that Elizabeth Gilbert brought out in *Big Magic, Creative Living Beyond Fear*.

Do you find solace or enjoyment in music, cooking, entertaining friends, reading or watching TV? I know one of the things I really missed was cooking after my husband passed away. He always loved my cooking, never complained and was easy to please. I missed watching, golf, football, tennis and our favorite shows together. It took a long time before I could watch any of the things we used to watch together. I couldn't even cook a meal without crying.

Life is about change

If there is one thing that I have learned over the years, it is that "life is about change." Nothing remains the same. I guess the big question is how we deal with change in our life. How do we survive change? How do we move beyond survival and prosper—perhaps in ways we never imagined.

I did eventually begin to watch football, golf and tennis again, but of course it wasn't the same without him. I started cooking again and inviting friends in for dinner. I still love to entertain but of course that's not the same without him either. But then, nothing remains the same. Every sunrise and every sunset are different, beautiful in their own way, each casting different shades of red, yellow, and blue. In the same way, each of our days is different.

My dear friend Krista just happened to give me Elizabeth Gilbert's book for my birthday. And she also started the chain reaction that led to me studying Qigong in Hawaii. It seems as with everything that Krista does, her timing is perfect. If we are to move smoothly through this life timing is everything.

*"Shoot for the moon and if you miss,
you will still be among the stars."*
— Les Brown

A Lunar Tool To Help Connect With Your Emotions

The Lunar Cycle is Like a Personal GPS

You can imagine my surprise when I was watching *CBS News Sunday Morning* and they mentioned how the moon impacts people's emotions. They said the moon affects the ocean tides and since our bodies are 75 percent water it's logical to believe it affects us too.

As a professional astrologer I have always been aware that the full moon is very powerful, impacts the way we feel, and magnifies everything that is going on in our life. Still, I was surprised to see it mentioned on the news.

The full moon puts things in our life under a microscope and forces us to see if we are happy with our life. We get clarity during the full moon. It's a time of self-analysis. It's a time to take personal inventory.

Through the eyes of an astrologer . . .

If you've never followed astrology at all, you might discover why so many people enjoy mixing it into their philosophy of life.

The many faces of the moon

Following the lunar cycle is perhaps my favorite and most reliable astrological timing tool. As the Moon travels from new to full it can be a tremendous aid for planning and timing events and understanding your emotions. The lunar and solar eclipses are especially "event and emotion" significant. The lunar cycle can give you a tremendous edge in your professional and personal life. It is without a doubt one of the major factors that is available in timing events to achieve your desired results.

The moon is about our emotions and how we feel. It affects how we react to emotional situations. And when the moon is full, it has a very powerful impact in the way we feel. It magnifies everything that is going on in our life. It puts things under a microscope and forces us to see if we are happy with our life. We get clarity during the full moon. It's a time of self-analysis. It's a time to take personal inventory. It is also a great aid to help us get in touch with and understand our emotions. I found it to be especially helpful as I was going through my healing journey. For example, when I knew we were approaching a full moon I knew that my emotions would be running rampant as if on steroids. I would find myself crying more and overreacting to my emotions. But then I would take a few deep breaths and remind myself that these feelings would pass. I also found meditation, Qigong, yoga, and exercise to be helpful.

Your personal GPS

Following the lunar cycle each month is like having your own personal GPS for your journey through life. The lunar cycle can be used in timing your activities and is one of the most valuable tools you can use. In many Eastern countries, timing by the planets is so important that practically no event takes place without first setting up an astrological chart. Many times, weddings take place in the middle of the night because that is when the planetary influences are the most favorable.

Since ancient times the cycle of the Moon from new to full to new has been observed and correlated with events on Earth. The early farmers learned that sowing seed at the New Moon leads to better harvest. Sailors learned to time their travels by the phase of the Moon, which everyone knows controls the tides. In addition to controlling the tides, the Moon rules the ebb and flow of the bodily fluids, emotions, feelings and state of mind.

Fishing and the Moon

Living at the ocean has given me first-hand knowledge of the trends of the fishing boats during the fishing season. Saltwater fishing is an occupation—or hobby—with a lot of self-anointed "experts" who often disagree with each other on just about everything, but catch records of professionals, recreational anglers and scientific studies say that saltwater species are more active for four days leading up to the Full Moon and for four days after the New Moon. There are other variables to consider, like water temperature and time of day, but when the Moon is full the trolling fishing boats light up the horizon like a Christmas tree. The tides are noticeably higher during the new and full phases of the Moon and the increased movement of water may hold the explanation for why the fish seem more active at this time.

Storm Patterns

At the New Moon, the Sun and Moon are together in the heavens creating a massive concentration of energy, which can lead to the development of strong storm systems. This can be an emotional storm or a full-blown hurricane. Think about how you feel when there is a Full Moon. Energy levels tend to run higher; less sleep is needed. The New Moon is the time to plant the seeds that you will harvest during the Full Moon.

Although the New Moon and the Full Moon and the few days leading up to them are the strongest times in the cycle, the total lunar cycle needs to be taken into consideration when timing an event or project. As I mentioned earlier, following the lunar cycle each month can be just like having a personal GPS to help you with your journey through life. It is a day-to-day guide for planning your actions and paying close attention to it will help you to better achieve your desired goals. Eclipse cycles can also add a strong impact on the weather, but that's the subject of my next chapter.

You will want to pay special attention if there is a storm approaching during a New or Full Moon. A perfect example that comes to mind is the series of hurricanes that hit Florida in 2004. I can still recall the weather forecast for the approaching storm as I was observing its daily movement in relation to the lunar cycle. We were approaching the New Moon of August 16 when Hurricane Charley, having come ashore on Florida's West Coast a little south of Tampa, was predicted to travel across the state and hit the East Coast of Florida.

We pulled down the shutters on our condo and battened down the hatches for what proved to be a thrashing, nightmare of a storm. In the pitch black of the night we could hear the shrieking sounds as the eye of the storm reached us and rushed over us. It has been said so often but it's true: it sounded like a fast-moving train rolling over our head. We were one of the few residents in the building who chose to stay and weather the storm.

I had survived Karen, a 210-knot typhoon when I lived on Guam, an island in the Pacific, while my father was stationed there in the Navy. I wasn't about to be chased out of my home by a hurricane that may or may not come our way. But it certainly did come our way. It was a doozy. Everyone in our building who did not have hurricane shutters lost their windows and sliding glass doors. Their interiors were left in shambles. All of the condo units located under these vulnerable units were also flooded as the water made its way through the ceilings and walls.

It seems that the condominium building located next to ours had a flat pebble roof and the pebbles where jetted through the air like bullets, destroying every windowpane that was not covered. Fortunately, our shutters saved us. Fortunately, our neighbors above us also had shutters which prevented us from being flooded from above. We were one of the few units that did not suffer water damage. Our storm shutters looked like they had been riveted with buckshot.

When we poked our heads out the door after the storm moved on, the parking lot looked like a war zone. There was furniture, debris and glass everywhere. It felt like we were in a bombed out, evacuated city and we were the only living souls around. It was devastating and brought back my childhood memories of typhoon Karen. In addition to the structural damage of the storm, the erosion of the shoreline was disastrous and heartbreaking.

Just three weeks later on September 8, 2004, hurricane Frances was forecast to be heading our way. Of course, we thought, no way, not again. When it seemed that "again" really was going to happen, I referred to my astrological calendar. This time the storm was six days prior to the September 14 New Moon, so I figured it would not be as devastating. We chose to stay, battening down the hatches once again. The biggest problem was that people had not had time to repair their roofs from the last hurricane and the water had not had time to seep into the ground. Unfortunately, the already damaged shoreline was getting another unneeded beating.

As if that were not enough, on September 26, 2004, hurricane Jeanne struck us. The Full Moon was September 28. She alone was not as destructive as hurricanes Charley and Frances, but she certainly added to the already disastrous situation. There was already way too much water and not enough time to repair roofs in between these lunar cycles. Of course, it goes without saying that we—and most of our neighboring communities—were without electricity for days or weeks. Some people didn't even get their electric turned back on before the next storm hit.

The lesson to this story is that you may want to consider evacuating if there is a major storm predicted to be heading your way around the time of a Full or New Moon. You can't stop it, but you can get out of its way.

Hurricanes are stressful enough when you have a partner to weather them with, but when the person with whom you had already weathered three storms is no longer with you, it's even more dramatic. Yes, with Hurricane Matthew approaching I guess I could have packed up and gone to Orlando and stayed with my son, but I decided to stay at the beach and weather it out with my neighbors.

Hurricane Matthew paid his visit in October of 2016. Fortunately, it was not a direct hit to our immediate area. As I was tracking its progress I wasn't too concerned since I knew it was not a full or new moon.

Your Lunar GPS: A Navigation Tool to help you work and connect with your emotions and what is going on around you.

I feel that I would be remiss if I did not share this information with you. You can easily learn to use the cycles of the Moon to help plan your activities so that you can enjoy optimum results. Most calendars provide this information. Of course, astrological calendars provide more in-depth information.

New Moon – When the Moon is traveling 0-45 degrees ahead of the Sun it is considered to be in its new phase. This is an excellent time to begin anything that you would want to have longevity. It is considered to be the germination cycle. This is an excellent time for putting ideas into action by initiating and outwardly directing your activities.

There is a direct correlation between what is already happening in your life and how you will feel and react to the energy of the New Moon. You may enjoy feelings of rest and peace if all is going well; or chaos, disorganization and confusion if your life is already in turmoil. Whichever is the case, whatever you initiate during this cycle should be fruitful. Just be careful. If you choose to do something harmful—for example, to initiate a campaign of revenge against someone—it may get out of hand. If you choose to begin a positive endeavor, it is likely to blossom. I chose this cycle to begin writing this book.

It is best to avoid elective surgery during this phase of the Moon, as there will tend to be more bleeding.

First Quarter or Waxing Moon – (seven days following the New Moon) When the Moon is 90-135 degrees ahead of the Sun it is still considered to be in the growth and development phase and activities that apply to the New Moon cycle also apply to the Waxing Moon.

Second Quarter – When the Moon is approximately 140–175 degrees ahead of the Sun the energy and activity is a continuation of the 1st quarter activities.

Third Quarter or Full Moon – (fourteen days following the New Moon) When the Moon is 180 degrees from the Sun it is considered to be in its maturity or fruition phase. This is when you will see the fruits of your labor and the seeds that you have planted during a New Moon cycle come to fruition. Emotions tend to run high. Depending upon what is going on in your life, you may feel ecstatic or depressed. Feelings and emotions tend to be exaggerated when the Moon is full. Elective surgery should also be avoided during this phase of the Moon as there tends to be more bleeding and swelling.

It has been my experience that people often times require less sleep or have difficulty sleeping a couple of nights before the Full Moon. Since energy levels tend to be higher, this is an excellent time to escalate your exercise program. You should be able to accomplish a great deal during this lunar cycle

Fourth Quarter or Waning Moon – (seven days following the Full Moon) When the Moon is traveling 90–135 degrees behind the Sun it is in its disintegration and drawing back phase. This is the time for reorganization, rest and reflection. This is when you will want to step back and get the big picture, to regroup and analyze your progress with initiatives you have already begun.

Balsamic Moon or Dark of the Moon – (fourteen days following the Full Moon) This is the 24-hour period just before the New Moon. During this phase of the Moon the Sun's light is not reflective. It is *not* a good time to initiate any projects that you would want to produce long-term results. This is also *not* the best time to be making new contacts, especially if you happen to work in the field of sales or marketing. This is also not the preferred time to sign contracts or legal documents as there may be a lack of clarity, or an inability to follow through.

This should be a quiet, working behind the scenes time. It is best to avoid high expectations, major decisions or physical projects. You will want to focus on mental tasks for the best use of your time on these days. This is a great time to plan and prepare for what you want to do when the Moon is new. Energy levels tend to run low during this cycle, so it's better not to push yourself.

The Moon Traveling through the Sun Signs

This is another tool that can be used to help you plan your activities in order to achieve a result that you'll appreciate.

I have found it to be very helpful to pay attention to the sign that the Moon is traveling through each day, as this can be a tremendous aid in helping you plan your activities. For example, when the Moon is in the sign of Virgo it is an excellent time for activities that require attention to details.

Since it takes the Moon two and a half days to travel through each Sun sign there is ample time for all activities in the course of a month. The Moon's movement through each of its signs can be followed easily with an astrological calendar.

It is also important to note on an astrological calendar that period of time when the Moon is *void of course*. The Moon is V/C (*void of course*) when it makes its last major aspect with another planet before going into the next sign. An aspect is the same as a connection to another planet. For example, the planet may be in the same degree and sign as the Moon or even opposite the Moon. It remains *void of course* until it enters a new sign, in which it will make another aspect. An astrological aspect refers to the relationship or connection between the planets.

During the V/C period it is advisable not to make any major decisions or sign contracts. It would be best not to start anything that you want to be long lasting. Think of it as a balsamic or dark of the Moon cycle. This can last for as little as a few minutes or up to several hours. Again, an astrological calendar will be instrumental in helping you chart your course.

It has been my experience that when the Moon is *void of course* it is very difficult to bring anything to completion, or even accomplish something as simple as reaching someone on the phone.

Observing the Moon as it travels from one sign to the next is like reading your personal barometer and acting accordingly. A barometer measures the barometric pressure in the atmosphere. It lets us know when the pressure is dropping and therefore rain is forthcoming. With that knowledge you can plan your activities more effectively. You probably would not want to schedule a picnic when the barometer is dropping. In the same way, as the Moon is traveling through each sign you can take advantage by timing your activities as they relate to the sign and task at hand.

Kelly Lowe

"Healing comes from taking responsibility: to realize that it is you, and no one else, who creates your thoughts, your feelings, and your actions."
— Peter Sheperd

Everyone Needs A Seed And An Inspiration
How Elizabeth Gilbert Watered My Budding Tree

Just as every tree needs its seed, I believe every writer needs inspiration. I believe that Elizabeth Gilbert was my seed, inspiration, and motivation. *Eat Pray Love* gave me the idea and desire to register for my retreat across the Pacific. Although the "Big Island of Hawaii" was an exciting and beautiful place to visit, and I was open to new horizons in my life, it was scary to think about embarking on a week-long adventure where I would not know a single soul except for the instructor.

As I wrote earlier, the trip turned out to be all I desired but even after I arrived at the retreat I continued to feel strong doubts and wanted to run from this new thing. Because I came to understand that great things often have costs, but paying that price turns out to be part of the prize you receive.

Embarking on a new adventure:
Feelings of trepidation and anticipation

My trip to Hawaii was so crucial that I'll risk repeating some of what I said before to tell you more about why it changed me. I've heard of people traveling joyfully to India to meditate at the base of the Himalayas and invite enlightenment into their lives, which they claimed to have found. It all sounded too easy. I went to Hawaii with great trepidation and anticipation. When I arrived at the Kona Airport, I looked around for Jeff the Qigong leader and volunteer chauffer. It was a very small airport, so I didn't have to wait very long, but there was a moment when I thought, what if no one shows up? What if I can't find him?

I did have his cell number, which I called and left a message. As it turned out there were two other women also waiting to be picked up. So we had a very enjoyable visit on the drive up the mountain to the retreat compound, which was beautiful. Meeting new people helped me relax and find a temporary escape from feeling alone.

There was an immediate sense of relief when I saw Jeff and climbed into his SUV. The front seat was full of wonderful island fruits and vegetables which I looked forward to experiencing. And I must say I was not disappointed with his chef's presentations.

When the two other women and I climbed into the SUV together there was an immediate connection, even though I had never laid eyes on them before. I could feel they were in Hawaii seeking their own version of what I was there for. We often meet people in life who are at points on their journey that are different from ours, but when we sense we are all moving in the same direction we know we share the same soul. This was indeed going to be a special week.

I quickly learned that Maya and Lee were also from Florida and they were planning to be married on the Big Island after the retreat. As it turned out, I became friends with them and I was invited to their wedding. I actually was their wedding photographer. I couldn't believe that I flew across the Pacific to meet people who lived only 150 miles from me.

As we entered the compound I was filled with awe at the natural beauty, open land and isolation. I was also overwhelmed by the feeling of isolation. There were twelve of us who had signed up for this once in a lifetime experience, but I was alone. I was not used to traveling alone. What in God's earth ever made me decided to do this.

I couldn't help thinking about the Hawaiian golfing vacation that Tony and I had planned years ago and had to cancel when my father was diagnosed with lung cancer. So this was a bittersweet trip. This was meant to be a healing trip. But was I ready for it?

My very first thought was to turn around and get on the next plane back to my aunt's house in San Diego, which was familiar to me. There I would feel safe and comfortable. Since we had limited cell service and limited power to recharge our phones, I was restricted in the calls I could make. But the first call I made was to my aunt to ask her if she could check on flights back to California for me.

Fortunately for me, they were very expensive and limited, so I was forced to stay on this beautiful paradise island for seven days "alone." I was someone who was used to being busy all the time, watching TV, emailing, internet connections, texting, calling friends, and having a couple of glasses of wine in the evening. This was all part of my routine. This would all change for the next seven days.

Once I gave in to my fate, it took me most of the first two days to decompress and appreciate what I was about to experience. I kept thinking about Elizabeth Gilbert when she was scrubbing the floors at the Ashram in India and sitting for hours in meditation in total stillness and silence. Yes, we also had quiet time at our retreat. And anyone who knows me, knows that I am not a quiet person. I love to socialize, and after my husband passed away I hated being alone.

Being alone was one of the most difficult things I had to adjust to. I was used to my husband being around almost all of the time, especially when he was so sick in the last few years before his passing—which was one of the many reasons I felt such a void in my life.

And now, here I was all alone in my cabin with a bunk bed and nothing else. Since the retreat was not full, I didn't have a cabin mate. I was left to my own space and my own thoughts except for the scheduled activities.

As it turned out one of the scheduled activities was hiking through lush, hilly tropical fields and across bubbling streams. Although the tropical fields were doable for me, I opted out because of the river streams. I didn't want to take a chance on reinjuring my quadricep tendon which had been repaired with major surgery a couple years prior to my husband's passing. It had been a very long healing and recovery process, and I certainly didn't want to take any unnecessary risks while so far from home.

And then there was the total hip replacement that I had two months after Tony's passing. No, I couldn't be hiking through any slippery mountain streams on this trip. So when everyone else went off on their hikes, I was alone at the compound with more time to meditate and think. It was a cram course in being alone.

It was now two weeks past the one-year anniversary of Tony's death and I was thinking that I should be feeling a lot better than I was about being alone. So I used the time to "go inside," to meditate and pray. I've always heard that praying is talking to God and meditating is when you listen to him. At home, before leaving on this retreat, I was neither talking or listening. Believe me, I wanted to, even though I knew it could lead me into places I was avoiding. That could have been it—avoidance. Despite living alone, I could always find some distraction—TV, phones, internet, anything—to keep me from meditating. I just was not able to quite my mind when I was home alone.

It reminded me of that movie "Home Alone" where eight-year-old, Macaulay Culkin, gets really busy and into all kinds of trouble when his parents left him home alone. It's not that I was looking for trouble; I just always needed to be busy.

This "alone time in Hawaii" was a true test of whether self-refection, meditation, and prayer were even possible for me now. Was I deluding myself by even signing up for this retreat?

It has always been my practice to carry a note pad with me and in this case I brought a fresh journal in anticipation of perhaps receiving divine guidance or inspiration to write during this journey. And that is exactly what I did. When I forgave myself for allowing my fears to almost overwhelm me, I began to realize I understood more than I gave myself credit for. Maybe I saw things that could help others passing through their own dark valley of loss. As inspiration emerged on the pages of my journal, so did the idea of writing this book. You might say it was born in the journal that I kept while I was there.

By the way, Elizabeth Gilbert's *Eat Pray Love* was also based on journals she kept while traveling through Italy, India, and Indonesia, although in her case the book wasn't exactly inspired *by* the journey. She imagined what the book would be before leaving on her journey and received a large advance from her publisher, which she used to finance the trip and write the book. Critics have questioned her work on that basis, but I believe there is inspiration in her pages. What I would say is that each of us must walk our own journey, but someone else's journey can help point the way. I hope my journey helps someone the way Ms. Gilbert's journey helped me.

So, there I was on the Big Island, left to my own devices without distractions or interruptions. As the evening breeze cooled my skin, the thoughts and feelings began to flow. My mind raced back to many years earlier when I was widowed the first time. My therapist told me to keep a journal and to write down five things every day that I was grateful for. That was one of the best pieces of advice about working through the grieving process that I have ever received. It worked then and it worked now in Hawaii. My thoughts and feelings began to reshape themselves—more hopeful, expectant of good things rather than full of fear that my best times were over. I began to smile as I wrote.

I discovered that naming things to be grateful for is a good practice at any time, not just in times of extreme emotional distress. To be honest, most of us suffer emotional distress at many points in our lives, and it might not even be tied to any single event. It might just come on all of a sudden. When it does, remember to make your list of things to be grateful for; it will help lead you out of darkness.

Over the years from time to time I've continued that practice. It doesn't have to be new things every day. I have found over the years that although I've added new things to my lists, I have continued to be grateful for many of the same things.

I have continued to be grateful for my wonderful son, grandchildren, aunts and extended family. My girlfriends are invaluable in my life. And of course, I am grateful for my good health and the ability to exercise and do something physical every day. After rehabbing from two major surgeries on my right leg within three years, I have a deep and imbedded appreciation for my ability to walk, swim, bicycle, do Qigong and yoga, play golf and live an independent life.

These are all things I took for granted until I realized I had almost lost them. These are all things that have continued to help me work through my healing journey. I say "work through" because I believe that we do have a choice as to how we want to proceed with our lives after a major change hits us—a change that we did not choose.

After suffering a loss or a major setback in life, we can pick up our marbles and go home. We can give up, which I believe we all do periodically and intermittently. But what is it that keeps bringing us back? What is it that gives us the motivation or the courage to continue when things get tough, when life goes off track?

Feelings of wanting to give up—
It's a Mortal Sin to commit suicide . . .

I still recall a few occasions when I couldn't chase away the thought of giving up on life and walking out into the depths of the dark blue ocean where the waves would carry me out to sea. It seemed like the answer or solution to the sadness and despair I was feeling. It would end my pain. But then I thought about the pain that I would be causing those that I left behind.

I was a hard-working divorcee, raising a young child, struggling to make ends meet when this deep, desperate wave of depression first swept over me. My parents had invited me to join them to visit some friends of theirs at their beach condo back in the early 70s. As I was walking alone along the edge of the shoreline, my thoughts were of escaping the pain.

Although I can't honestly recall the exact trials and tribulations that I was going through at that time, I knew that I was very depressed and felt unable to cope. Sometimes a series of smaller setbacks can drain our strength of spirit as surely as a large challenge like the loss of a loved one. So that evening I seriously considered allowing the waves to engulf me, to swim with the fish and the dolphins. Although I was a fairly strong swimmer and my parents would probably not have believed that it was an accident, I figured that a few gulps of saltwater would sweep me out to sea. Obviously, this was not a very rational thought process and probably would not have been a very peaceful or desirable way to leave this planet.

There were two things that held me back. Although my son was very young at the time and my parents adored him and would have raised him in my absence, I couldn't leave that stigma on him for the rest of his life. I have always believed that having my son saved my life. God does work in strange and interesting ways. He always seems to send us what we need, when we need it most. Alex is my only child and I don't know what I would have ever done, or would do, without him.

Since no one really knows what happens to us when we leave this world, I meditated on that a great deal, and still do for that matter. I was raised Catholic and was taught that it is a mortal sin to commit suicide. So if I did decide to check out early I would be doomed to eternal damnation in hell—whatever that is.

Reincarnation . . .

I had also studied and learned about reincarnation—not in the Catholic Church, of course. This is the belief that we have to keep coming back to a physical life on earth until we get it right. It is the belief that this life is not our first rodeo, which is why some people are more talented in certain areas then others. I believe that we all come into this life with certain talents and how we choose to use and develop our gifts is up to us.

We have been here before and done it before. Take Beethoven for example; he is the most obvious manifestation of someone who came into the life with an extraordinary talent and gift. There's no other explanation.

So, in other words we have to keep coming back until we get it right. I've always had this feeling or belief that if we leave this world miserable and unhappy, we have to come back and deal with those feelings and issues in the next life.

I know it sounds crazy and there is no evidence or proof of this that I know of, but it is a theory that kept me from walking into the ocean many years ago—that and the stigma that it would have put on my son. Then there is the Catholic Church's teaching that suicide is a "mortal sin" punishable by eternal damnation. Intellectually, I didn't believe this, but as other Catholics have said, the church's ingrained teachings can be hard to overcome.

I guess I wasn't too far gone mentally if I could walk on the beach and do all that rationalizing. Of course, no one really, really knows the ultimate answers, but it's certainly something to think about. I've also studied and read about people who had near death experiences and their stories are compelling.

So why am I bringing up these deep rooted, depressing memories from years ago when I was divorced? Because I believe that the emotions and feeling that we experience when we lose our spouse through death or divorce can be very similar—even when we are the one who wants the divorce and believes that is necessary. I needed to remind myself of that. I have witnessed many friends recovering from both kinds of loss and I've seen that in either case the hurt was persistent and genuine.

In the months that followed my husband Tony's passing I walked the beach a lot and had those very same feelings and thoughts. I wanted to just walk out into the waves and allow them to engulf me. I thought about how long it would take before my lungs would fill and I would be overtaken.

Of course I didn't think about it for very long, or even very seriously. Because again, there was my son to consider and now I have grandchildren whom I adore and would never do that do. Then there is reincarnation and the "mortal sin" thing to think about. Yes, sometimes we can boost our spirits by recalling the things we are grateful for; at other times exploring the downside of our actions can help us right our ship.

As I said before, no one really knows, but I do believe that we are all here for a purpose, and until our creator decides that it is time for me to move on, I need to keep seeking my purpose and working on this great gift of life I've been given.

I've always felt that my purpose was to share information and make a difference in other people's lives, which is what motivated me to become an astrological coach, write my first book, this book, my monthly newsletters and my Facebook posts. What exhilarates me and keeps it all fresh is that my eyes open a little wider all the time as my understanding of the human condition continues to grow.

Life is about change and adjusting to the change and I have always found that astrology was a great tool to help me understand and work with the changes. I should say astrology and my belief in God. I believe that God created heaven and earth and all the planets. I have learned and experienced that studying the movement of the planets as they affect all of us living on planet earth is a very helpful and important tool.

Astrology and writing, my works of love . . .

In her book *Big Magic*, Elizabeth Gilbert wrote that whenever anyone tells her that they want to write a book in order to help others, she always thinks, "Oh please don't." She wrote that it was much better to write a book to entertain and help yourself.

She talks about the book she just happened to write based on her travel memoirs while trying to save herself after a failed marriage. Little did she know then that it would turn out to be a best seller and a very popular movie. I know her story certainly made an impression in my life. I can still remember when I read the book and couldn't wait to see the movie. Although I was in a good place in my life at the time—my husband had not been diagnosed yet—I still appreciated and could resonate with her story.

Everyone who hasn't been living on Mars or Venus knows it was called *Eat Pray Love*. I've seen it several times since the original release in the theater and have found something new in it every single time.

So, Elizabeth Gilbert's theory, which I totally agree with, is that if you do whatever it is that you love doing and it feeds your soul, it may end up, inadvertently, helping others. Elizabeth shared these words of wisdom from the theologian Paul Tillich, *"There is no love which does not become help."*

Ms. Gilbert also wrote, "If you can't do what you long to do, go do something else. Go walk the dog, go bake a peach cobbler, go paint some pebbles with brightly colored nail polish and put them in a pile. You might think it's procrastination, but—with the right intention—it isn't, it's motion.

And any motion whatsoever beats inertia, because inspiration will always be drawn to motion. Do something. Do anything."

This got me thinking about how I have actually been doing this most of my life—looking for answers for myself that eventually became answers for others as well. I started studying astrology in the early 1980s at about the time when home computers became affordable and popular. If had not been for being able to calculate the astrological charts on a computer, I would never have pursued this career. It just made life so much easier. So as I pursued the career that was calling me, I found that the tools I needed to make it work seemed to appear. People talk about "being born at the wrong time," well I believe I was born at exactly the right time. Born in the right place at the right time—all of us have a better chance at living a joyful, fulfilled life if we believe that.

As I have become more and more evolved and conscious of what I have learned and shared over the years, I feel very rewarded and deeply satisfied with my life's journey and my work.

The interesting thing is that Larry, my first late husband, was very supportive and encouraging about what I do. As a result, my career evolved quickly. I was thriving in my work—reading for clients all over the country, teaching classes at the local college. There was a featured article about me in the local newspaper. I had found my niche and what fed my soul. I truly loved what I did and the people that I was blessed to work with.

A few years after Larry passed away, I met Tony, who was very conservative. He really wasn't very keen on the idea of dating an "astrologer," which is probably why it took us five years to get married. Eventually I slowed down with my astrology work and he became more tolerant of what I did. But our life was busy, and my work took a back seat. Still, during this time I continued with my practice and when the time was ripe as Tony convalesced at home, I wrote my first book, *An Astrologer's Journey*. And now in the aftermath of Tony's death comes the inspiration for my new book.

When you reach for what you love doing, all good things are within your grasp. Prevailing winds are always in your favor. That's what happened at the retreat in Hawaii; once I stopped resisting, the winds carried me exactly where I needed to go.

"It all works out in the end. If it isn't worked out, it isn't the end." — Traditional Wisdom

Connecting With Your Sun Sign

Light a Path to Expanding Connections

Everyone is looking for a connection—it's all about feeling connected and, as a result, feeding your soul. Astrology is another tool to help us get connected and find out what feeds our soul.

I have found astrology to be an invaluable tool to help people overcome and deal with loneliness and depression. Astrology can help you appreciate and understand how you connect with other people.

It occurred to me when I was working out at the gym one morning and I saw a guy wearing a Gator shirt and shorts. I thought, he wants everyone to know that he is a Gator fan, which I happen to be too, so I smiled and said, "go Gators." He smiled back and we made a connection.

My grandson was wearing an Atlanta Braves baseball hat one day when we were out shopping and a guy in the store said, "Looks like we finally have a team this year." The Braves were seven games up in first place at the time with a good chance of making it through to the World Series.

And then there are the fan clubs in the music word, people who are connected by enjoying the same artist or group. For example, I have often thought about connecting with a Jimmy Buffett fan club, also known as "Parrott Heads." I still might do that someday. And with social media it is so easy to connect with any artist fan club that you could possibly want.

I have a friend who connected with the Leon Russel fan club after her husband passed away and she travels all over the country for their social events. She said they have become like family to her.

Then there's the coffee clubs and wine tasting connections. Starbucks certainly has created a niche for people to gather and socialize. Not that I am a big Starbucks fan, but I do notice that they seem to attract a lot of people who enjoy connecting on a regular basis to drink coffee and share stories.

Have you ever noticed how many wine tastings clubs there are? This also seems to be a popular social outlet.

As a student and practicing professional astrologer for most of my adult life, I have found astrology to be an invaluable tool. It has helped me to better understand myself and those around me, and to more effectively coach my clients.

Each sun sign has its own personality, and so, accordingly, each individual has their own way of dealing with loneliness and making a connection. This may explain why some people have more of a need to interact and make a connection than others.

This is what I have observed and experienced in working with my clients, friends, and family members over these many years:

The fire signs—Aries, Leo and Sagittarius, and air signs—Gemini, Libra, and Aquarius, tend to move forward at a quicker pace if they experience a setback.

The water signs—Cancer, Scorpio and Pisces—tend to withdraw, internalize and process their feelings. While the earth signs—Taurus, Virgo and Capricorn—tend to move in a slow organized direction. They will analyze and assess their financial situation to make sure they are secure.

Aries tend to have a pioneering, independent, competitive attitude. They especially like to move fast. They won't let any grass grow under their feet. If there is a way to fast forward feelings of depression or loneliness, they are all for it. They are all about going full speed ahead. It doesn't mean that they don't feel the pain, they just have to keep moving while they are feeling it.

They feel better if they hit the ground running in the morning instead of lying in bed thinking about the past or feeling sorry for themselves. There's no time for self-pity for an Aries. Some people may think they are insensitive or lacking in emotions, but the truth is they mask their pain with activity.

Since they are by their very nature a pioneering spirit, they are always up for starting and trying something new and different. This can be their salvation and greatest healing tool when dealing with a loss. I am not suggesting that they wake up the next morning after experiencing a loss as if nothing has even happened but staying busy and having a plan of action is a terrific antidote for them.

Taurus natives tend to be patient, steadfast, and conservative. On the other hand, unlike Aries, they tend to slowly process the change and let go. They will first want to access their financial situation and stability. They are slower to deal with and accept changes in their life, especially the loss of a spouse—even when the handwriting is on the wall.

They find that working helps them to maintain stability, to stay grounded. They can find comfort in gardening and or just being in touch with nature. Those who were born with their sun or moon in the sign of Taurus usually find healing comfort when they have plants or flowers around them.

Fresh flowers can play an important role in the healing process for everyone, but especially for someone who has their sun or moon in Taurus. They may find comfort in food and may need to be careful about the extra pounds.

Geminis tend to be literary, versatile, adaptable, analytical and curious. This is another sign who likes to keep moving and get on with life. They find comfort and healing through connecting and interacting with their friends. Most Geminis are avid readers. They tend to be students of life. Reading about dealing with loss can be very healing for them. It is also helpful for them to journal, write, and share their experiences.

Cancers tend to be nurturing, receptive, cautious, reserved, and persevering. Family is everything for a Cancer. The loss of a family member, even an elderly grandparent or distant cousin, can be devastating for them. There is a tendency for them to hold their emotions inside with outbursts of tears of emotion. One of my Cancer friends said she invariably cries at weddings and funerals. Their deep sensitivity can affect their sleep pattern, their appetite, and their attention span. They find comfort in staying close to their home environment when grieving. Since they are initiators and activity oriented, home projects can be very healing for them.

Leos tend to be generous, ambitious, creative, entertaining, and optimistic. They need to let the child in them come out to play when they are dealing with a loss—let their creative juices flow. I can recall one Leo client who enjoyed painting, and after her husband passed away, she painted the most beautiful landscapes. She even sold a few through a local studio.

Virgos tend to be ingenious, witty, studious, and methodical. They find comfort and stability in being organized and tending to the details of closure. They need to feel needed. They need to have projects and structure in their life.

Libras tend to be persuasive, tactful, intriguing, social, charming, and can be indecisive at times. They usually find comfort and condolence with friends and social activities.

They cannot bear to feel like they have fallen into a well that they cannot climb out of. They do their best to create or manifest some balance. Social media can be a superb tool for creating and maintaining social and emotional connections which promotes the Libras' need for connection as long as they don't overdo it.

Scorpios tend to be private, introspective, and very deep in their emotions. Although counseling could be very helpful for them, they may find it difficult to open their emotions and let go. It's not easy for them to show or share their deep feelings, so it may take them a little longer to work through their feelings.

A friend of mine was dating a handsome, charming Scorpio man, but feared it would never work out because of his past. He had come home from his father's funeral to find another man in bed with his wife. They had a two-year-old little girl who meant everything to him. He had thrown his whole being into making a life for his young family. His reaction was to punch the intruder and file for divorce. He left a very good job and went on the road driving a truck for a major transport company. He took his little girl with him when school was not in session, and they listened to classical books on tape as he drove the highways. The daughter was now in college, and he had never re-married and never really gotten over the pain.

Sagittarius can be the eternal optimist and prefers to look at the glass half full rather than half empty. They are also the bachelor and bachelorettes of the zodiac. They can enjoy traveling and being outdoors, especially if it is a trip to an exotic place they have never been before. Sagittarians are the philosophers of the zodiac and can also be religious minded. A spiritual quest may be in order for some Sagittarians while they ponder life's lessons.

I have a Sagittarian friend who, after her husband left her, traveled to Egypt all alone from Florida to join up with a tour group of mostly Australians to cruise the Nile, explore the pyramids, and look for ancient symbols. She was overjoyed to find the Flower of Life in an ancient temple ruin and came home feeling much better.

Capricorn — When it comes down to brass tacks, Capricorns can put their *big boy* pants on and become all business. Although they can feel lonely and disconnected, they tend to channel it in a productive, structured manner. There's no self-pity party for a Capricorn. Granted, they have their moments where they break down in private, but for the most part they put up a pretty good front.

I can still recall when my father passed away after a very short-lived lung cancer diagnosis. My mother, a Capricorn, worked with the help of a widow friend and family members to immerse herself in dismantling and preparing to sell their 30-foot motorhome. Capricorns tend to be great at organizing and delegating. Even when grieving, they can reorganize their life and make a plan of action.

My parents had traveled from Florida to Alaska, through Canada to Nova Scotia and all the states in between over a period of twenty years. They enjoyed a wonderful life together. But the task of dismantling their home on wheels was a monumental project which my mother embraced almost immediately. It gave her a focus and a purpose. Work and projects can be a great healing and growth avenue for Capricorns.

Work is a great antidote to help Capricorns through challenging times. Like Aries, they do better when they are staying busy, although they do tend to be more organized and tenacious than Aries.

Aquarius tend to be inventive, intellectual, diplomatic, and independent. They find comfort in social or humanitarian activities. They need to have a plan of action and set their goals. They enjoy their independence and like to do things their way. They can usually find a unique and different way to process their healing journey.

Pisces are intuitive, compassionate, introspective, loquacious, and clairvoyant. They have more of a tendency to want to withdrawal and escape. Sleeping is an excellent healing antidote for them. When a sweet Pisces lady lost her husband to a heart attack, she hardly got out of bed for a month. Then, a friend and silent business partner of her late husband offered her the opportunity to run the art gallery her husband had started. She threw herself into re-opening the gallery and spent the rest of her life fulfilling her late husband's dream.

Feeling lonely, depressed, or disconnected is okay as long as we know how to process and deal with our feelings.

If You're Ready For An Ambush Is It Still An Ambush?

Celine Dion Says Learn From It, Use It

Again, just about the time you think you are healed and have all the tears and sadness behind you, something pops up that brings on another swale of tears. It doesn't have to be a major event. But for some reason holidays do seem to be a trigger.

It might not be a major holiday, like Christmas. It could be Memorial Day or 4th of July. As my neighbor said to me when I told her about my emotional setback on Memorial Day almost two years after Tony passed away, "Holidays are family times and when a family member is gone the void is most glaring on those days. Memorial Day weekend is when Tony and I would usually watch the French Open tennis tournament and the Indianapolis 500 on TV. I tried to watch the French Open alone, but it just wasn't the same without him.

My friend Joann who facilitates a bereavement

group at her church told me that feeling sad is okay. It means you have great memories. You're remembering the good times and the fun you had together.

My housekeeping is a direct reflection of my emotional state of mind

In addition to being great exercise, you can't cry when you're swimming. I have discovered that cleaning is also a good antidote and therapy for tears. I don't know why but there seems to be a calming and sense of satisfaction when I start vacuuming. I especially enjoy using my "Shark" steam cleaner on my tile floors. Now I know why I enjoy cleaning.

I recall watching an interview on TV years ago in which Celine Dion said that she enjoyed cleaning her own bathroom. She said she grew up dirt poor and this kept her humble and in balance. It was good therapy. She said it made her feel good. I thought that was kind of odd at the time, considering all of the fame and money she had. She could afford ten housekeepers, but she said it kept her life in perspective. This made me wonder how Celine Dion dealt with the death of her husband from cancer on January 14, 2016, only six months after Tony's passing. Then her brother, only 57 years old, died of the same kind of cancer two days later. I could picture the two of us seeking solace from our pain—me vacuuming and Celine on her knees cleaning her bathroom.

> **I believe that knowing you did the very best you could to care for your loved one is half the battle of moving forward.**

It seems that cancer has no financial boundaries. It doesn't care if you are wealthy and famous or poor as a church mouse.

Losing her husband of 21 years, René Angélil, to cancer in January, 2016 didn't come as a surprise, as he had been ill for some time; but as the Grammy-winning artist herself said: Her family lived with hope even when there was no hope. And she claimed to feel stronger after Rene's death, perhaps because she believed he would always be with her.

Dion took a leave from her Las Vegas show in August 2014 to devote herself to caring for Angélil, who in addition to being the father of her three children had been her manager for the entirety of her storied career. And understandably, though it was valuable time spent together, watching his condition deteriorate was also a very painful experience.

"I proved to Rene that he was there for me and I'm going to be there for him—and I'm still there for him," Celine said in her 2017 interview with Natalie Finn at eonline.com. "I took care of him the best way I could."

I personally feel and believe that knowing you did the very best that you could to care for your loved one is half the battle of moving forward. At first there was that feeling of maybe I could have done "this or that." Then come the thoughts of *if only* ... I experienced those same thoughts and feelings when my mother passed away and both of my husbands. There was always something that I wish I would have said or done. And from what I have learned that's pretty normal.

The reality is that we all do the best we can.

When our loved one is gone, I don't believe they look back in judgment. I believe they are in a better space and a better place. This may sound a little cliché but if there is individual consciousness in the afterlife, I have to believe it is a consciousness of pure love, not one of petty grievances—either imagined or real.

The first year after losing her husband, Celine said "love, faith, family and unsinkable strength" were her comfort. They had started out as a professional relationship—he served as Celine's manager—which later turned romantic leading to a lavish wedding in 1994.

As Celine continues to get used to her new normal, the Grammy winner is revealing some of the final words she shared with her husband. "When he passed, I stood by his side and I said, 'You know what, it's okay, you know you didn't deserve to suffer that much.' He was cold. I said, 'It's enough, it's enough of suffering. You gave so much, you don't deserve that,'" she explained. "I said, 'I'm fine, the kids are fine, okay, everything is going to be okay. You taught me, you taught me well. I'm going to use it.' And that's what I do every day—so Rene will never die."

Although we are not all Grammy winners, I believe we can appreciate and be inspired by Celine Dion when she made an emotional return to the stage in Las Vegas, just over a month after her husband René died while battling throat cancer. In addition to her husband's death, Dion's brother, Daniel Dion, died two days after Angélil.

The singer honored her late husband of over 20 years with a moving montage of photos and video that can be seen on her website, celinedion.com. As reported by Carly Ledbetter of Huffpost, the tribute also included an emotional message. "I understood that my career was in a way his masterpiece, his song, his symphony," said the text in the tribute. "The idea of leaving it unfinished would have hurt him terribly. I realized that if he ever left us, I would have to continue without him, for him."

The singer teared up a few times during that first night back on stage and broke down during her signature song "All by Myself." She finished the night in true professional fashion with the crowd totally on her side.

"Don't cry because it's over, smile because it happened." — Dr. Seuss

Reaching Back To Rediscover Your Strength

*We all Need "Go-To" People to
Help Validate Our Worth*

It has been and is my feeling that there is a great deal of comfort and satisfaction in reconnecting and revisiting.

In my former life, many years ago before I met my husband Tony, I was director of sales and marketing at a resort in Stuart, Florida.

It was during this cycle in my life that I took a Transcendental Meditation (TM) class and began the practice of daily meditation. I was introduced to the work of Edgar Cayce, one of the most prolific psychics in the twentieth century. I studied Tarot Cards, dream analysis, and numerology in addition to continuing my astrological studies. I was a true seeker, and in many ways I still am. There's always something new to discover.

And then came an exciting breakthrough. I met a woman named Betty Riley who helped change my life. She was a psychic medium who had written a book called *A Vale Too Thin – Out of Control*. Her true experience of reincarnation is one of the best documented cases on record. Without going too deeply into Betty Riley's story, she was a psychic of remarkable ability whose awareness of past lives manifested in her present life.

I know many people find such phenomena hard to believe, but those people have not met Betty Riley. Her ability to see things far beyond the limitations of most people was so powerfully real that university researchers sought to find a viable explanation.

So when Betty saw something in me that I had not seen in myself, and encouraged me to pursue my astrological gifts, I knew that my path had been chosen.

And, as I envisioned taking my life's work to a higher level, I also understood that the thing which made it a higher level was the opportunity for helping and working with others.

I continued to thrive with my love of helping others through astrology. My studies and practice continued to grow. Then I met Tony. As wonderful as he was, he had reservations about me being an astrologer, which is why we dated for five years before we got married. Eventually he began to learn and understand more about what I was doing. He understood that there was not a conflict between God, religion and astrology. So we were able to live happily ever after until ...

Of course, given the central role she had played in my life, I reconnected and reached out to Betty Riley after Tony passed. She lived in Atlanta and I lived in Florida, so we were only able to talk on the phone, which I found to be very comforting.

Although we had always kept in touch through email and phone calls, I hadn't seen Betty in over 20 years. When she told me she was going to do her "swan song" in Milwaukee, I immediately said "I'll be there!" I had previously done an astrology program for the Edgar Casey group in Milwaukee, which is where she would be speaking.

I loved the group and knew that reconnecting face to face with Betty after all of these years was going be invaluable and instrumental in my healing journey. It was everything I hoped it would be. I scheduled a reading with her which was very enlightening and helpful.

> **She said it's important to let the ego go when meditating. Shut everything down. Just allow the mind to be quiet and listen.**

I found it very interesting that it directly correlated with the information that I was seeing in my astrology chart. She didn't tell me anything that was foreign or uncomfortable to me. One of the things that she told me that struck a chord with me was that I should write another book. She actually validated that I was on the right track and path with my healing journey.

I believe we all need validation in our life no matter how strong or confident we are. And we should all have our "go to" people. Our "go to" people can be different people at different times in our life. And quite often they get as much from giving to us as we receive from them.

As I have said before, I believe everyone is in our life for a reason, even if it is only a season.

Thank you, Betty Riley for being in my life. My "go to" person was a mentor in the field which I made my life's career. Yours might be someone different according to your beliefs—maybe a pastor, or former professor—someone you respect who isn't necessarily a close personal friend.

During Betty's workshop she mentioned that when she lived in Florida many years ago, she would always walk on the beach when she was searching for answers or looking for comfort. She said she believes in God and, "when I look at the magnitude of the ocean my problems seemed so small." Her belief in God is what got her thought the tough times.

She also believes in the importance of meditation and makes it a practice to meditate daily. When you pray, you talk to God, but when you meditate, you listen to God.

She said it's important to let the ego go when meditating. Shut everything down. Just allow the mind to be quiet and listen. Granted this does take practice, but it does develop with time and patience. Some people find it easier to meditate when they are walking. They say walking quiets their mind. Betty says just do whatever works best for you.

One of the books that Betty Riley referred to during her presentation in Milwaukee was Ruth Montgomery's *How to Communicate with Spirit*. Ruth Montgomery was a journalist with a long career as a reporter and syndicated columnist in Washington, DC.

Later in life she became a celebrated psychic and author of numerous books on spiritual subjects. During the 1960s and '70s Montgomery became a regular on the morning talk show circuit, and was for a time a household name. She was a pioneer that helped make Betty Riley's career possible.

One of the things I have learned from my studies is that if you can imagine it, you can reach it. Don't let someone else's beliefs limit you—whether it is an individual, an institution, or the culture. The most rewarding path is always the one you choose for yourself.

Of Friends and Lovers

When You Need to Bond, Think First of Friends

As I reflect on where I have been on my path and consider how I have connected with so many fellow travelers on my life's journey, I am in constant amazement and appreciation of the dynamic effect that girlfriends can have on helping us through this process. I don't know what I would have done—or would do now—without them.

The loving support and connection with family is certainly very important, but as we get older most of our children take on a life and responsibility for their own family, spouses, children, and careers. They haven't stopped loving you, but they are at a different time of life, busy maintaining and running their own households. To put it simply, they are writing their own family narrative in which you are an important character, but not the lead role.

I have known people who never had children for whom friends become more like family than many families. Girlfriends often seem to form an exceptional bond, especially after they lose their spouse. Maybe that's why widows don't seem to feel the desire or need to remarry as quickly as widowers do . . . or do they?

You may have heard the saying "widows mourn, men replace." It sounds like common sense. If it is true, no one had actually proved it so, or explored why it might be that way.

We're all aware of the demographic imbalance between men and women, but is there more to it? I found a fascinating article called *The Desire to Date and Remarry Among Older Widows and Widowers* by Deborah Carr at Rutgers University that specifically tries to answer three questions about later life match-ups: (a) Do widowed men and women differ in their preferences for dating and remarriage in the short term (6 months) and longer term (18 months) following spousal loss? (b) To what extent can the observed gender gap in re-partnering be explained by gender differences in the perceived benefits and strains of romantic relationships, compared to other forms of social support? *and* (c) Is the fulfilled (or unmet) desire for a romantic relationship associated with psychological adjustment to spousal loss?

The entire research-based article, which is easy to read, can be found at *http://www.rci.rutgers.edu/~carrds/publications/remarriage.pdf*

Girlfriends in times of transition and reconnecting

In some ways the article can only tell us what the numbers say about how people behave after loss, what is the most common outcome. But "the numbers" don't have to predict what happens to you. It is my belief and experience that we can design our own outcome. One thing you can count on is if you don't design your life yourself, someone else—or circumstances—will design it for you. That sounds a little scary.

I'm not saying you should picture yourself as a lone wolf bravely crossing the horizon on a high ridge. No, we all need companions—co-conspirators if you will. I have been very fortunate in that I consider myself to be a very healthy and independent person, but there was an occasion a couple of years after my husband passed away that I found myself in an emergency situation when I developed a pinched nerve in my upper back. This is probably the most excruciatingly painful experience that I had ever experienced, next to shearing my quadriceps tendon a few years before my Tony passed away.

The difference with the sheared tendon was that Tony was with me. I never felt alone. I was in a great deal of pain, but I wasn't alone. And that was important to me.

When I made the trips to the emergency room with the pinched nerve drama, I was fortunate and blessed to have my girlfriends' support. It was as if the universe saw I was in need and knew just who to send to help me.

I can still recall years ago while I was married to Larry, who was suffering more and more from congestive heart failure. I could see the handwriting on the wall but didn't have the kind of close girlfriends I could turn to. Perhaps it was a life habit from my youth. Growing up as a military brat, we moved every two years, so I never really developed lifelong girlfriends. It was during this time in my life, as Larry's health slipped away, that I decided to join Beta Sigma Phi, a professional sorority.

As my husband was going in and out of the hospital, I felt a strong need for bonding with girlfriends. I didn't let that feeling pass without acting on it. And I can say now that decision to act set off a chain of events that ended with some wonderful lifelong girlfriends. I don't think I could have survived without their love and support over the years. Of course, my parents were always there for me, but they too have passed on.

What I keep my eye focused on now is not who is missed and gone, but rather who is here. I do appreciate the friendship and support of my girlfriends.

And then you meet someone . . .
If you're hungry, here's food for thought

After months or years of "being alone" and enjoying your time with your "girlfriends" you meet someone special. He fits your intention list. He's the answer to your prayers and dreams. So, what happens to the connection that you had with your girlfriends? This has the potential to get a little sticky, I feel that I'd be remiss in not addressing this issue.

One example that comes to mind is a friend who fell off the face of the earth when, after five years of being a widow, met the man of her dreams. Although I was very happy for her, I missed our connection and friendship. As great as her marriage might have been, wouldn't she have been even richer if she continued to nurture the love and friendship of girlfriends?

Life certainly does change when you meet someone, but what happens if it doesn't work out and you've kicked all your girlfriends to the curb. I guess that's why I feel it is important to keep a balance in your life even when you think you have met Mr. Wonderful.

Girlfriends are forever and, well, men seem to come and go—for whatever reason, no matter how long they stay. At least that has been my experience. So don't lose touch with your girlfriends no matter how wonderful "he" is. And, of course, sisters can be best of friends. The following quote, author unknown, is from a Valentine's Day card I once sent my sister:

> *"She not only shares in your past,*
> *But she shares in your future plans;*
> *She's not only a great companion,*
> *She's one of your greatest fans ...*
> *She is your sister friend."*

It takes as long as it needs to take before moving forward after a divorce, the death of a spouse, or any loss. There is no magic formula.

New Beginnings After Divorce

The Price of Reconnecting

Opportunities for change and growth come in many forms. Of course, the most final is when a spouse or loved one passes on, but a divorce is also a loss—especially if it was not your idea. Oftentimes, there is a victim and a villain when there is a divorce (and there might be disagreement over which is which).

The divorcee or divorcer is still around. The feelings may linger for an extended period of time. There may always be the thought that you could get back together, or guilt about what you could have done to save the marriage Death, on the other hand, is very final.

In the 2005 academy award winning movie *Sideways*, which I saw during a girls night out at our local Cinematique, we enjoyed the adventurous trip through the Santa Barbara wine region by two buddies—a handsome soon-to-be-married actor

Jack Cole, played by Thomas Haden Church, and a down-on-his-luck divorcee Miles Raymond, performed by Paul Giamatti.

Although Miles has been divorced for five years, he can't get over his ex-wife. He keeps thinking they are going to get back together again until he runs into her at his friend's wedding—along with her new husband—and finds out that she is pregnant. He finally gets the message and decides it's time to move on. He goes back to the wine country and hooks up with a woman he met there who was very interested in him. It took being slapped in the face by the facts, but he was finally able to move forward with his life.

> **In listening, speaking up, and honoring your truth, you will know when you need help**

I think what resonated with me was that it takes as long as it needs to take before moving forward following a divorce, the death of a spouse, or any other loss. There is no magic formula.

Having gone through both a divorce and the loss of two husbands, I could certainly identify with this movie.

* * *

If there is a formula, although probably not a *magic* formula, the closest I have seen is the blog by Family and Marriage Counselor Wendy Crane. With her permission I am sharing her article on transforming one's self after going through divorce. I've summarized the major points here.

In the article she details four steps to a happier you. The first step, Wendy writes, is acknowledging that loneliness is not solved through a relationship with someone else (I'd like to see this in a block), because, as many of you know, sometimes the deepest loneliness actually occurs within relationship. It is resolved through remembering that your foremost relationship is with Y-O-U! This is the second step. If you are in a partnered relationship, the relationship you develop with yourself will serve to enhance and deepen how you share yourself with your partner.

For the third step, she says to remember we are derived from a much greater source of energy than we could ever imagine and staying connected with that *source*—which is comprised of *love*—fills the hole within you that we often call "loneliness."

No human person can do that for you. As a great and wise teacher once reminded me: "When you are alone, you are *with yourself*." So, as the fourth step, Wendy says if you want to overcome loneliness, it's time to cozy up with you and only you.

How can I develop a deeper relationship with myself, you ask? Here are 10 ways Wendy Crane says you make it happen:

Listen: Do you ever notice or hear a little nagging sensation or voice within you that seems to guide you toward the next step in your life? It may nudge you to make a change, try something new, or bring something to a close. It always starts low and subtle and if unacknowledged, can develop into a loud, screaming obstacle that will not move until you choose to pay attention. This is your inner knowing, often called intuition, your soul, or your Truth. Part of strengthening your relationship with yourself is about trusting this inner voice and heeding its call. Become an active and attentive listener to the part of you who seeks your highest good. The more you trust it, the more clear your life path becomes, and the less opportunity you have to abandon yourself. If you choose to stop abandoning yourself, loneliness dissipates.

Honor and respect your Truth: These are the actions that follow once you have chosen to listen to and trust your *Self*. If you want others to honor and respect you, you must begin with honoring and respecting *you*. If you consistently throw yourself under the bus, apologize for your existence, or minimize your experience, you deny the truth of who you really are. If you honor and respect what feels true for you, you will set better boundaries, receive more love and feel supported. It is difficult to feel empty when you are taking good care of yourself.

Be patient: Take it easy on yourself. Rome was not built in a day. Oftentimes, you may have internalized messages or experiences from childhood that cause you to set up walls of protection and patterns of disconnecting from yourself in order to survive. Deconstructing your walls and developing patterns of connection and trust within yourself through the first two steps, can take time and practice. This becomes your "work." This process is often part of the life lessons you are here to learn. Your challenges become your teachers. Take your time to allow the learning to heal you.

Speak up: Use your words. Tell the truth. Say only what you mean and mean what you say. Do not agree to something that causes your stomach to churn or feel uneasy (that is a clear sign you are surrendering your power and abandoning yourself). In the speaking of your Truth, you honor yourself and those around you; you develop trust that you can count on yourself to advocate for what you need and ask for what you want. Release fear about expressing yourself—you are worth speaking up for. The more you love and value yourself, the easier it will be for the words to come out.

Develop a spiritual practice: You come from a great *Source*. What name you call that *Source* is not as important as your relationship with *It*. The relationship between you and your *Source* is what a spiritual practice nurtures. This is where prayer, meditation, yoga, service, time in nature, mindfulness, music, art, and creativity come in. Engage in activities that help you feel connected to something much bigger than you. Practice humility, surrender, and experience grace. When connected to this energy of love, allow it to permeate all of your cells and fill you up. When your whole being is filled with love, it is very difficult to also feel lonely at the same time.

Do something nice: Just as you would in a traditional relationship, be thoughtful. When there is something that comes up that you know you would like to do, take yourself. Watch the movie that you've been wanting to see, cook foods that nurture you, update your home or wardrobe to match your new outlook, take yourself for a walk or get some extra sleep. This is all about taking care of *yourself*. Identify and give yourself what you need in this moment. Believe that you deserve it and allow yourself to receive.

Hug yourself: This is another gift to give yourself. It might feel funny at first, but it feels good!

Be mindful of what you feel when you give yourself this type of positive attention. Notice how different it might feel from other types of attention—such as judgments, pressure, and self-rejection.

Say "I love you" (A LOT!): When you are getting ready each morning, take a moment to look into the mirror, look right into your own eyes and say, "I love you, I love you, I love you." Really see yourself, see beyond the surface and all the imperfections, right into your inner-being—the one who tries and who makes mistakes, and who works so hard. And before you go to sleep each night, take one more moment to really see yourself and say, "I love you. Thank you. Tomorrow is a new day." Feel free to add in other times as well. Do this every day for thirty days and notice what happens.

Ask for support: When you need help, ask. You don't need to create a crisis, drama, get sick or throw a temper tantrum in order to get others to notice that you need help. In listening, speaking up, and honoring your truth, you will know when you need help and will find the words that you need to ask in a clear, concise way.

Play: When you allow yourself to shed the armor of adulthood for periods of time, you allow that inner-you to come out and play. Get down on the floor and play with a child, run and jump in a park, play with your pet, be silly, laugh, or choose a workout style that is more playground than machines. Giving yourself permission to play allows you to get in touch with your creativity, vulnerability, and passion. Get to know this part of yourself—it has much to teach you.

It is my personal sincere feeling and believe

that this advice is applicable for moving forward after the loss of a spouse through death as well as divorce, as both losses can create a sense of loneliness. Thank you Wendy for allowing me to share . . .

For more helpful information about Divorce Recovery visit Wendy Crane's website. You can download the full article free and find other helpful information. https://www.solflowerwellness.com/divorce-recovery/

"We are the sum total of our experiences. Those experiences—be they positive or negative—make us the person we are, at any given point in our lives." — B.J. Neblett

By Our Thoughts All That We Are Came Into Being

At Least That's What the Buddha Said

I have said several times now that I've always believed there is no such thing as coincidence. The older I get, the more I see and appreciate the magic some people call synchronicity. It's not just that an extremely improbable "coincidence" occurs in a life, it's that the occurrence speaks deeply to the person in some important way—a kind of revelation of who you are. Maybe another way of explaining this is that you attract what you think about, as Ernest Holmes and Willis Kinnear wrote in, *Thoughts Are Things*, which is why it is always important to have productive, healthy thoughts.

So, if you are trying to connect in a meaningful way—friendship, colleague, or romance—thoughts become manifestations. Everything that happens begins with a thought. I can recall thinking after my husband passed away that I wanted to get involved in some type of volunteer work. My first adventure volunteering was working one afternoon a week as a receptionist in my church office. That was okay for about a month, but then I started to lose enthusiasm. Something always seemed to come up that I needed or preferred to do on my volunteer days.

I finally realized that perhaps this was not the type of volunteer work that I was meant to do. So, I had to come up with something else. I thought about volunteering one morning a week at the hospital gift store. A friend of mine organizes the volunteers at the store and she invited to me to sign up. But once again I had to make a commitment for a specific day and time every week. I felt fairly sure that, as happened with the church office, other things would come and get in the way. I guess that's why I never wanted to go back to a 9-5 job after I was able to get away from it.

That's probably one of the many reasons why my work as an astrological counselor and author has suited me so well all these years.

Which brings me to my next "magical thing." While exhibiting at an event one evening, I met a representative from one of the assisted living retirement homes in my area. When she suggested that I might come and do a program for their residents, the idea grabbed me. This could be the volunteer work I was searching for that would feed my soul. I was excited about it in a way I never felt with the other volunteer positions. I could schedule the program at my convenience, and I wasn't committed to a weekly schedule and time commitment. And I would be doing something that I love to do. I would be entertaining and sharing my passion. I would be giving these people something else to think about—at least for a while. My plan was to help brighten their day.

So my first program was scheduled and presented to a room full of very senior citizens. I couldn't help but thinking about my own mother when I walked into the room. She always enjoyed social activities and a room full of people. And she always enjoyed my talks when she was able to attend. She was my biggest fan. She came to my first book signing and was so proud of me.

I got so much more of what I wanted as a volunteer from sharing my programs at the nursing homes and retirement centers.

It was such a pleasure to interact with the residents and see their faces light up as I talked about their sun signs and the lunar phases. I shared with them some basics on how the lunar cycle affects our emotions and how people tend to be more emotional when there is a full moon. I loved seeing their faces light up as they realized that they had felt this full moon effect themselves.

Although most of them may not have grasped everything I was saying, I noticed that when I talked about their particular sun sign they would perk up and pay attention. They even began to ask me questions about their children's sun signs.

It seems that everyone enjoys hearing about their sun sign, even if they are in an assisted living facility or a nursing home and have never really thought about astrology before. I certainly enjoyed sharing that information with them.

I eventually returned to volunteering at the

hospital when they had an opening on their auxiliary board for a public relations chairman. This was right up my alley. I enjoyed working with the other volunteers and I felt connected and I didn't have to work on a set schedule. I also trained to be a substitute receptionist in the hospital lobby, which also did not require being on a set schedule.

Opening myself to volunteering has opened me to becoming a new person, changed from the person I was before my husband became ill, and certainly from the person I had to be after he passed. It was a wonderful way to connect. The universe has given me opportunities that have lifted me up and added to who I am, like a building rising up story after story.

As B.J. Neblett wrote in his book *Quotable Quotes*, "We are the sum total of our experiences. Those experiences—be they positive or negative—make us the person we are, at any given point in our lives. And, like a flowing river, those same experiences, and those yet to come, continue to influence and reshape the person we are, and the person we become. None of us are the same as we were yesterday, nor will be tomorrow."

"Any motion whatsoever beats inertia, because inspiration will always be drawn to motion." — Elizabeth Gilbert

Volunteering:
A Proven Path To Connection

Find Your Passion, Find Meaning

The area in which you volunteer need not be anything at which you are skilled, or one that provides a service—just something you enjoy.

One of the first things I did after my husband passed away was to sign up as a volunteer at golf tournaments. I had often thought during our marriage about doing that but didn't want to take the time away from "us" to go off and spend several days volunteering.

As Elizabeth Gilbert wrote in her book *Big Magic, Creative Living Beyond Fear,* "Any motion whatsoever beats inertia, because inspiration will always be drawn to motion. Go walk the dog, go pick up every bit of trash on the street outside your home, go walk the dog again, go bake a peach cobbler, go paint some pebbles with brightly colored nail polish and put them in a pile. Make something. Do something. Do anything."

Although she is referring to developing your creativity I also believe and have found that this is a great antidote for grief and coping with depression and feelings of loneliness. I chose to become more actively involved by volunteering at golf tournaments. Although this may not be everyone's cup of tea, it helped me to fight back the tears.

My husband and I enjoyed attending many professional golf tournaments together over the years. When I first met him, I was a neophyte to golf. I knew nothing. I actually knew less than nothing because what I thought I knew was all wrong! But since he was such an avid golfer it seemed like a fun thing to learn to do. So I decided to learn the game and started taking lessons.

Yes, it is frustrating at first, and can be a frustrating game in general, but it's also wonderful and exhilarating when you get a good shot and see the ball rising and sailing down the fairway. And there's always that hole in one to look forward to—which I'm still looking forward to but not giving up hope. I was playing with a gal when she did get a hole in one and that was very exciting for everyone in our foursome. Maybe I'm next!

My first golf related volunteer job was at the LPGA course in Daytona Beach, a home course for the Ladies Professional Golf Association. The event was the Symetra Tour Championship. The Symetra tour is a national, professional, women's golf tour that calls itself the "road to the LPGA." Top performers on the Symetra qualify for the "big tour," so this is serious business for the golfers. I drove a golf cart taking the players and their caddies from one hole to the next, which was fun. Some of gals were very chatty and others very serious and quiet. But they were all very pleasant.

The weather was great, and I was out enjoying the fresh air which took my mind off my loss. It was something I had never done before. It was a part of my healing and growth process. I was all about doing new and different things and enjoying new experiences.

I was spreading my wings as I was growing and healing. After working the women's qualifying tournaments a couple of times, I decided to branch out into golf's big league.

My husband and I had visited the Torrey Pines golf course in La Jolla, California, years ago. Although we weren't able to play golf there at the time, we always thought that we would someday. They have two beautiful and challenging courses. We always enjoyed watching the men's Professional Golf Association (PGA) Farmers Open tournament on TV. It is played Torrey Pines every February. TV does not do the courses justice. They are much more beautiful than they appear on TV.

So after putting a few local LPGA tournaments in my resume, I decided to be brave and sign up online to volunteer at this major event. My husband had passed away in June and the tournament was the following February, so it gave me something to look forward to. Having "something to look forward to" is always good. And traveling was at the top of my list of things to do during that first year. That is, as soon as I recovered from my hip replacement. (Yes, I had a hip replacement two months after my husband passed away. But that's another story!)

Since my aunt and uncle lived in San Diego, this trip would be a double pleasure. I planned to go out and have a nice visit with them and enjoy the new experience of volunteering at a major PGA tournament. Life was good.

But wait a minute before you start to envy me. When I arrived for my assigned volunteer job, I discovered that it wasn't exactly what I thought it was going to be.

You see, I signed up online through the volunteer site to be a "shuttle driver," which is what the job was called that I did at the LPGA tournament in Florida. As it turned out the "shuttle" I had signed up for at the PGA tournament meant I was to drive players to and from the San Diego Airport.

I said "are you kidding me?" I don't drive on the California Freeways. Everyone knows they are notorious and only the locals dare risk it. It seems that I totally misunderstood the description of the job on the website. I thought shuttle meant driving the players around the golf course like I did for the LPGA tournament in Florida—a great way to spend the day—not battling the tense jam-ups of California freeway traffic.

As it turned out the only player shuttles that are used at Torrey Pines are to take the golfers from the practice putting green area to the practice driving range at the top of a big long hill. This is the job that I wanted, that I thought I was signing up for in the first place.

I guess if I had been a local resident that would have been the end of it. They'd have said "tough luck Kelly, maybe next year." But when they learned I had flown all the way from Florida to volunteer at this event, they said they'd see what they could do about getting me into the inner, closed circle that drove the players from the putting green to the practice range. It seems that committee is pretty tight and made up of people who've worked together for years. I was told it is very tough to get a spot as a "golf cart shuttle" driver.

But as luck, or God would have it, I was able to meet with the chairman who was in charge of that team of volunteers and he managed to fit me into their schedule. So I got to meet and drive the big name golfers around, and watch them practice up close. Unfortunately Phil Mickelson didn't ride the shuttle. He used his personal cart and driver. It was a memorable experience but would have been more memorable if I had gotten to drive Phil. I did get to watch him finish his round on Friday, but he didn't score well enough in the first two rounds to make the cut and go on to play the weekend that year.

The weather was perfect the days that I worked, but it turned very nasty the last day of the tournament—which I was not scheduled to work, thankfully. They had to suspend play and finish on Monday. That was the year that a horrific storm came through and uprooted many of the beautiful trees, totally changing the terrain and appearance of the course.

The weather in La Jolla that time of winter, which is always when the "Farmer's Open" is played, can be beautiful or terrible. And sometimes it's both on any given day. That's California in February.

When my aunt asked me if I was coming back the following year to volunteer for the event, I told her that once was enough. It was a wonderful and memorable experience. I got a very nice hat, golf shirt and windbreaker as a part of my registration fee, which I am continuing to enjoy. I totally appreciated and enjoyed the experience, but I wouldn't ask my aunt and uncle to make the morning commute to La Jolla again. The traffic was ... well, I'll just say you have to experience it to know what I mean.

And while I'm at it, I'll just say thank you Aunt Jeannie and Uncle Frank for all that you have done and do for me. I couldn't have made it thought that first year without you. I would add that when any of us are recovering from loss it isn't easy to let people get near enough to see our pain—even when they are close family. I was glad I resisted that impulse. Seeing other hearts filled with compassion can be our invitation back into the world.

Although this was a trip of a lifetime for me—to be a volunteer at this major PGA Tournament—It was bittersweet. I always thought that I would be watching this tournament with Tony. But I felt that working at that tournament was one of the turning points in my healing journey. At some moment you just have to step off the curb and cross the street alone, without the beloved partner who had helped give life purpose. I felt a full gamut of emotions, as I reflected on our trip to California the first year after we met. We had a wonderful time visiting my aunt and uncle in San Diego and drove up to Torrey Pines to see the golf courses.

Life tends to be a roller coaster during the times of loss and adjustment. There was the anticipation during the flight out there, the disappointment of not having the job that I thought I had signed up for, and sadness of not having Tony there to enjoy watching the tournament with me. Not that he would have been a volunteer—that was not his thing. But he would have enjoyed being a spectator. He so loved golf! That's the thought I held on to as I returned home to Florida.

I have continued my volunteer work on a local level, serving on the board for the LPGA ARG Daytona Beach Chapter and have become active with the Advent Health Daytona Beach Auxiliary, as I continue to feed my soul.

> *"If you're in a bad situation, don't worry it'll change. If you're in a good situation, don't worry it'll change."* — John A Simone Sr.

Did Someone Say It Would Be Easy?

When the Unthinkable Happens

She was married to her best friend and drinking buddy—someone she could laugh and have a good time with. Then the unexpected hit him. He contracted hepatitis C. He stopped drinking. He stopped smoking. He stopped laughing and they stopped having sex. He became a completely different person. Their life totally changed.

In her mind, he was still her best friend and she was more than willing and happy to take care of him. And after all, she was a Pisces. Of all the zodiac signs, Pisces are perhaps the most inclined to be caregivers, and Virgos are right there with them. That's probably why we find so many of them in the healthcare profession.

Although she had a full time job that was really more than full time, she devoted herself to taking care of this man who had been her husband and best friend for over twenty-one years. She saw him through his darkest days and into his recovery. He beat the hepatitis C with her by his side. She was, by all measures, a compassionate caregiver.

Just about the time she thought the worst was behind her, the unthinkable happened. She was diagnosed with small bowel cancer, which is very rare and very aggressive. The survival rate is less than five percent. I first met Mary when she attended one of my astrology workshops. I had just learned that my husband had been diagnosed with the very same cancer. I couldn't believe it when she approached me after class and told me. What are the chances of that happening?

She shared with me that she had already been through the surgery and treatment and was in remission and doing great. This was very encouraging and gave us a ray of hope. She was one of the very fortunate five percent who had survived. She was very supportive and a good friend through my husband's five-year battle, even though, as it turned out, he was not one of lucky ones—the one in twenty who would survive the cancer.

Unfortunately, when Mary was diagnosed, her husband said he couldn't "do sick." He was not a caregiver and didn't want to be married to her any more. He had met someone else and wanted a divorce.

So her life became an out-of-control roller coaster ride. She felt like she was flailing. She didn't know where to turn, so she threw herself into her work, trying to masque her hurt and disappointment in this man whom she had taken care of during his time of need. Sometimes life just isn't fair and this was certainly one of those times. She was devastated. She was beginning to wonder if the sun was ever going rise again.

Just about the time she had reached the end of her rope, dangling over the pit of despair, a friend told her that she needed to pray about it. She had proven she couldn't handle it on her own so it was time to seek help from a higher source. It made perfect sense to me. Yes, we need to do our own part of the work, but we don't have to do it all. The simple words we so often hear are more than a cliché: "Let go and let God."

So as she was driving home from work one day, her phone rang. It was the higher source calling her. Actually it was her mother who lived in another state telling her that the house next door to hers had become available and suggested she consider moving back to her hometown. She literally picked herself up, dusted herself off and moved back to live next door to her mother.

She was very employable and it didn't take her long to land a nice position in her new location. A new life was being born. As Jimmy Buffett sings, "Changes in Latitude, Changes in Attitude."

Now she is back in her hometown, divorced and on the dating scene at age fifty-three. Dating wasn't new to her, but it certainly was different than when she was thirty-two. She met what she thought was a really nice guy in a neighborhood bar. He was cute and there was definitely a spark between them. They talked for hours the first night they met.

Mary had been given advice from a friend about the things you shouldn't talk about when you meet someone for the first time: Don't talk about your divorce. Don't talk about politics. Don't talk about sex. And don't talk about religion. Of course within twenty minutes they had covered all those subjects.

After four hours of getting to know each other, he walked her to her car, kissed her goodnight and said he was going to call her. He never did. She learned later from someone who had seen them in the bar that he was not the most stable guy in town. So she had dodged the proverbial bullet, avoiding a first post-divorce relationship that was doomed from the start. She never heard from him again.

Maybe there was a better way to meet someone, she thought, and decided to go on *Match.com*. She was motivated. After all, she was only fifty-three and really wanted to meet a nice guy. She actively worked at it, which I've heard is what you really need to do if you're going to date online. You have to check your hits every day and reach out to anyone you think is interesting. It's a numbers game. I actually know a lot of people who have met Mr. or Ms. Right on those sites and ended up happily married to them.

Mary did date one of her "matches" for eighteen months, even though he never told her he loved her—which bothered her. She wanted more, so she finally asked him how he felt about her after all their time together. He said he just wanted to be "friends with benefits." Well, that didn't work for her at this stage in her life.

So, on the heels of their breakup she was working a trade show out of town when she ran into an old friend whom she had known years earlier while she was married to her "best friend." As it turned out, while she was single he was now married—of course unhappily—but married nonetheless. And, of course, there were too many complications, mostly financial, for him to get a divorce.

He was, however, able to help her professionally through his business connections, so they managed to take quite a few trips together. And of course, she fell in love with him to no avail. This lasted about a year before she just couldn't take it anymore. Again, life was too short to be so miserable.

This is when she decided to "order a new one" on the internet. She had a little more experience now and knew what she wanted—and especially what she didn't want. She had kissed a lot of frogs up to this point. She had taken care of her husband through hepatitis C and survived small bowel cancer. She made a major change in her life by moving back to her home town and landing a dynamite job. Now, at age fifty-seven, it was her turn to find happiness with the right man, which is exactly what she did—or thought she had.

She moved back to Florida where she really enjoyed living and went on line with a whole new profile and outlook. She was being very cautious as to what she wanted to attract. She had her priorities in order and after a short search she thought that she had found Mr. Right.

Of course, there's always a few things you'd like to change, but for the most part he was perfect for her. He played the guitar, he was nice looking and funny, and most of all, he adored her. Now she is really enjoying the sunrises.

Unfortunately, Mr. Right had a few flaws in his armor and skeletons in his closet that took her by surprise. The flaws and incompatibilities started surfacing right around the 90 day mark. In astrology, 90 days is when a new relationship can be expected to move to a different level and take on a different tone or complexion. It either advances into something better where the couple will feel even closer, or they start to drift apart or end it right then.

In this case major health issues were one of the skeletons in his closet. He was not a healthy person, which she learned through several trips to the emergency room. It was not long after their 90-day mark that he made his final trip to the ER. It wasn't until after he passed away that she discovered he was married—separated, but still married. Regardless, Mary grieved his passing and needed time to sort it all out. Fortunately, she was able to benefit from bereavement counseling.

Following her divorce years earlier, Mary never doubted that she would date again. But now, having followed that path through several twists and turns, she could testify that dating after fifty is definitely not for sissies.

So once again she picked herself up, dusted off, and jumped back into her very demanding, high profile job. After all, she told herself, life had been very fulfilling and busy before she met her now departed love. Mary hadn't changed her mind about love, nor did she harbor regrets. She still believed it is more fun to have someone to share sunrises and sunsets with. She hadn't given up on meeting Mr. Right on a dating sight, but decided to take a break, knowing that the sun always rises. Who knows, Mr. Right could show up on one of her sunrise beach walks.

In my practice and in my personal life, I've seen the many paths friends and clients have traveled as they dealt with loss and feelings or loneliness and disconnection.

Other Voices, Other Stories

Conversations With Women Who Have Discovered What Feeds Their Soul

I learned a long time ago that I needed structure in my life.

So when I begin to feel depressed or disconnected, I find solace, security, and comfort in planning and organizing structure in my life. The first time I was widowed, I started training for triathlons. That would be mini-triathlons of course, half-mile swim, twelve-mile bike ride, and three-mile run. But still, at fifty years old that wasn't too shabby. It made me feel good about myself and helped me grow physically and emotionally stronger to deal with my loss.

I also immersed myself in my work. I began seeing clients again, teaching and doing workshops again. And I taught an astrology course at the local college. I enjoyed living a very structured and fulfilling life.

So when I was once again widowed, after the initial shock I dug down deep to reconnect with what I needed to do to find my "new normal." Yes, even if you know the person is not going to survive their illness, there is still a period of shock when they make their transition. So once I had regained some sense of balance, I became very structured in my workout routine. I did not see any more triathlon training in my future, but I did join a new gym which offered more classes and equipment in addition to the Olympic size pool I had been enjoying at the YMCA.

Once again, I immersed myself in my work and increased my schedule of doing workshops and seeing clients. Since I had written my first book during my husband's chemo treatment and recovery, I decided this was the time for me to allow the new book growing inside me to come out into the light of day. Everything I had experienced since writing *An Astrologer's Journey* was making me stronger, feeding my soul, and giving me a level of wisdom I hadn't known before.

As I began imagining the new book in conferences with my editor, I also branched out in my local community. I joined and became active in my local Chamber of Commerce. I joined the Yacht Club, where I grew excited about resuming my astrological talks there which I called "Dinner with the Stars." I joined the local Travel and Ski Club. Although I am no longer able to ski, it was a great social outlet and helped to reconnect with that community.

Loss in Our Time or Our Time of Life

In my practice and in my personal life, I've

seen the path many friends and clients have traveled as they dealt with loss and depression. Sometimes I am able to help them, and on many occasions I have learned from their experiences. It seemed like there was a lot of that—meaning recovery from loss— going around at about the same time my husband passed. And of course I started to energetically attract clients who were going through the same thing.

I learned through our conversations what it was that they did to feed their souls in those challenging times in order to move forward with their new normal. What helped them to grow and find themselves again after their loss? I've added their revelations to those I experienced myself.

Joann's Story

Reinvention Goes More Than Skin Deep

Joann was always very active in her church, so when her husband, Jim, developed Parkinson's and passed away after seven years of her lovingly caring for him, it was only natural for her to become even more involved in her church. She said she found comfort and strength in her connection with God. Without her faith she could not have made it through. She knew in her heart that he was home again with Jesus and he would no longer be suffering. This was a certainty in her heart and mind, and it gave her solace.

Although she was free of the considerable care Jim required every day, like many caregivers before her, she had a hard time embracing this as freedom. Instead, she felt that she had lost her job and purpose after Jim's passing. She set about finding a "new normal" that didn't include caring for Jim. She first joined a bereavement group at her church to help her through the initial shock—and she stopped doing things that no longer suited or served her.

She was involved in a direct marketing company that was very time consuming and unrewarding, but she had been inspired to work at it while Jim was battling his disease. She let go of that and soon found a niche, a purpose that fed her soul and was more rewarding. She and Jim had been greyhound rescue parents for years, but when they lost their dog Bo during Jim's illness, they decided not to adopt another greyhound. It was just too much in addition to taking care of her husband.

Then, about a year after Jim's passing, she became a foster parent to Lizzie, a three-legged greyhound who she ended up adopting. In addition to making Lizzie her own, she accidently fell into becoming a pet sitter, which has truly been her niche and calling. It started with friends and neighbors and grew into a full scale business which she loves and is very good at.

Oh yes, not very long after her loss she decided to have some cosmetic surgery which took twenty years off of her appearance. Now that's what I call reinventing yourself and finding the "new normal."

Finally, she has become a facilitator for the bereavement group at her church. She said she gets so much more than she gives and this truly feeds her soul and spirit.

How Sylvia Was Restored By Faith

Believe That Anything Is Possible

Sylvia and her husband Gene owned and operated a health and fresh produce store in my neighborhood. The store is on my way home from my morning rituals at the gym. I enjoyed stopping a couple days a week and visiting with them while picking up my vitamin supplements or anything else I needed to help address any issues that that might be affecting my body at the time. And their fresh produce are the best—much better than my local chain supermarket.

Not only were they warm and friendly, hardworking and caring people, they were very knowledgeable in homeopathic and natural remedies. They were always willing to take time to listen and assist customers with whatever remedies they could offer. I can remember one morning talking to Gene about being awake all night with leg cramps. He immediately directed me to the some magical potion of apple cider vinegar, natural ginger, and garlic juice. It tasted horrific, but oh my God, did it ever work!

That's just one of the many times Gene came to my rescue. He was a natural at helping people and anyone who knew him couldn't help but love him.

Transition

Right around the time that my husband was going through his cancer treatment, I walked into their store one day and learned that Gene had also been diagnosed with cancer and was going through treatment. I had thought he looked to be losing weight and was a little fragile, but you would never have known it by his attitude. He was still as warm, friendly, and caring as he had always been.

Even after his treatments began, whenever I asked how he was doing he would always say "great." He was optimistic, positive and always showed the appearance of beating it. But he was looking more and more frail as time progressed, until finally one day he was no longer able to come into the store.

Family members started pitching in to help keep the doors open while Sylvia, Gene's wife, was spending more and more time with him at home. And then hospice was called in. I kept asking about him, knowing that one day I was going to get the bad news. It finally came about nine months after my husband had passed away.

I felt awful for Sylvia and the family. Not only did she lose her husband, but she had a business to try to save. She had to make a living. As anyone knows who has lost someone, especially a spouse, things begin to change as soon as the diagnosis is delivered. And when you're trying to make a living and run a business along with dealing with the illness, it can be overwhelming. But somehow they managed to keep the doors open.

When I spoke with Sylvia I could see and feel that she had a strong spirit and faith. She was determined. She told me her faith in God—and a life beyond this one—is what saved her. She said she felt close to Gene when she was at the store.

The "vultures" starting circling immediately after the news got around that she was now a widow struggling with a business. Although she didn't want to sell the store, she was being encouraged to let it go. The struggle with Gene's illness and passing had no doubt set the business back. But the store was still a part of Gene, and she did not want to let go of it.

She and Gene had been married for 33 years. They met while working at an A&P grocery store. Over the years they had owned and operated several different businesses together, so she was not a foreigner to the hard work that it takes to run a small business. And she was a person with a good head for business. Although she had all these things going for her and did not want to let the store go, she was talked into listing it with a realtor. Almost immediately after Gene passed a lowball offer came in. She was sick about it, but encouraged to accept, which she reluctantly did. She wasn't thinking clearly, but down deep in her heart of hearts, she knew she wanted to keep the store. She prayed about whether she should follow through with the sale.

Sylvia has a very strong faith. She said that in her life, "God has first place." She has read the bible all the way through twice, but is not a bible thumping kind of a person who demands that you see things her way. When I asked her about her religious beliefs, she said, "Religion is man's idea of God's expectations of us." She believes that the most important thing is to, "Love God, love yourself and love your fellow man—and with this all things are possible."

She shared this passage from the bible with me. She has memorized the words and repeats them every day. She said this has gotten her through losing Gene.

Proverbs 3:5,6

5. Trust in the Lord with all your heart and
lean not on your own understanding:
6. In all your ways acknowledge Him,
and He shall direct your paths.

Her prayers and faith were answered. As it turned out the offer to buy the business did not go through for various reason which I will not go into. But in her heart of hearts Sylvia knew that her prayers had been answered. She told the realtor to take the store off the market. She knew she had a lot of work and praying to do to get the store back on its feet and to catch up on the bills. It was a struggle, and without family, friends and the community pulling together to help her, she could not have made it.

Then just about the time she was beginning to see the light of day, seven months after Gene passed away, Hurricane Matthew hit us. It flooded the store. The entire community was pretty devastated by the storm. It was sad for me to drive down the street and see all the store fronts boarded up.

But once again Sylvia's faith came through for her. She knew that God was going to take care of her, and he did.

Someone told her about FEMA, the Federal Emergency Management Agency, the government organization that helps small businesses after a natural disaster, as well as homeowners. She had to apply by filling out tons of paperwork and jumping through a series of hoops, which she was willing to do. The love that she and Gene shared, and the passion they both felt for the health food business, kept her going. The business was a part of Gene and she did not want to let it go. And she believed that God was with her every step of the way. And so, it turned out, he was.

With the help of her FEMA loan and the support of her family, friends and community, she was able to get the store up and running once again. She and her "team" personally repainted, redecorated, redid the floors, and generally revitalized the store. As a regular customer I can attest that the store and Sylvia are going stronger than ever. Once again, her faith had seen her through.

Lisa's Conscious Decision To Move Forward

No One Can Do It For You

Lisa had always been a very self-sufficient, independent lady. She enjoyed cooking, sewing, gardening, reading, and always allowed time to keep up with her tan by the pool. She especially enjoyed her pets. She always had a dog and a cat to care for, and when she met Bill after being divorced for nine years, he fit into her life perfectly. He was a gem. She enjoyed and appreciated the wonderful relationship that they had together. They enjoyed traveling together, going out on Friday nights and knowing they could talk together about anything. For Lisa, having Bill to bounce her ideas off was wonderful.

When he passed away after a long battle with prostate cancer, she was devastated. Due to family circumstance and complications, she was forced to sell their home. Her life was going to change drastically.

After selling her house in the city, she started a new life in the "country," near where her very good friends lived. She told me she had made a conscious decision to move forward. "No one else can do it for you," she said.

At 72 years old she chose to start a new life in a new place and moved to a small retirement community and who would have thought that she would meet a very special, wonderful man there. It had been two and a half years since her significant other had passed away, when one evening she was at a dance with a girlfriend whose husband was out of town. It was a perchance fluke that Lisa was even there that night. She had never before been to the dances that happened on a regular basis at the new community, but thought "why not" when her girlfriend invited her.

It just so happened that sitting across from her that evening was a very nice looking, interesting gentlemen who asked her to dance. She quickly found out that it was also his first time at one of the dances. His wife had passed away two months prior and it was the first time he had been out to a social event. They enjoyed a delightful evening, and he invited her to dinner the next evening—which led to them spending a lot more time together.

She soon learned that he was a devout, traditional Catholic who believed that having sex out of wedlock was a sin. She, on the other hand, was not really into traditional religion. Was this to be the deal breaker? No, not really . . .

Who would have thought that she, now 74 years old, and he, at 81, would once again find love. After almost a year of dating and spending a lot of time together they decided they wanted to spend the rest of whatever time they had left on this earth together. I guess the moral to this story—and reason they wanted to share it—is that we're never too old to find love and have a relationship, if that is what we want. She shared with me that she now goes to church with him—which was something that really surprised me!

> *"Where attention goes energy flows. What you place your attention on blossoms and blooms, and what you drift your attention away from withers, diminishes and dies."*
> — Davidji

Two Years Later, Life Continues

Acknowledge the Blessings

The first anniversary of Tony's passing was spent visiting family in California and then on to the spiritual Qigong retreat in Hawaii I have shared with you. I wanted to just escape and run away for the first anniversary and in many ways that was exactly what I needed to do. And as fate would have it, the retreat became a springboard into the rest of my life.

But the second anniversary was different. I chose to stay home in the home that Tony and I had shared. I wanted to embrace and acknowledge his impact and blessings in my life and the lives of his family.

So when I extended the invitation to our family to gather for a cookout at our home, it was unanimously accepted. They too wanted to celebrate and acknowledge the major role that he had played in our lives.

We laughed, we told stories, we looked at pictures, we remembered the good times we shared with him. His sister Linda, who had known him the longest, of course had the best stories. But her most cherished memories were about our trips to Las Vegas together. She explained that she never sits down at a blackjack table without hearing her brother say, "Linky, (his nickname for her) you gotta take a hit on 16 . . . ." She loved her big brother, as we all did.

My life is certainly different after moving forward through the first two years following Tony's passing. It was a journey that only I could travel with myself and for myself. I carried with me all the wonderful memories which I cherished, along with the company of my family and friends who are very near and dear to me.

As I spoke with other widows, I discovered that many of them felt the same way that I did. They did not feel that they needed another man in their life to make them happy. They were happy and content in their own space. If someone absolutely wonderful came along they might reconsider, but they were not hitting the bars or doing *Match.com*—not that there is anything wrong with that. It just didn't suit the needs for the woman I spoke with. Most of them were enjoying doing their own thing in their own way, just as I had learned to do.

After my husband Larry passed away in 1992, I made myself a list of what I wanted in a relationship. Some of the things remained the same when Tony passed away in 2015, and some were very different. The list was definitely longer. I called it my "intention list." I set my intentions with the energy of a "new moon," exactly as I have taught and described in my chapter about using the lunar cycles. My list was specific about what and who I wanted to attract.

I kept the list next to my bed so I could re-read it on every new moon and reevaluate to make changes or updates. I have always found this to be a positive way to manifest my desires. I tried to be as specific and detailed as possible. In addition to my list, I prayed that when the time was right and my heart was ready, the right man would come into my life again and I would be ready to appreciate him.

Although that is certainly not a priority for me at this time in my life—and my intentions list keeps evolving—I always keep an open mind and continue to enjoy every sunrise.

One never knows where you might meet someone. It's usually when you least expect it, but I believe it is important to set your intentions, as with everything in life.

> **So I've come to the conclusion that the first and most important thing in life is to find peace and happiness within—essentially to be happy with yourself and allow yourself to believe it.**

I can recall many years ago, when I was a young woman, reading *The Power of Positive Thinking* by Norman Vincent Peale. Unfortunately the copy with all my handwritten notes did not make it through my many moves over the years, but the message I took from the book has remained. As I worked my way deeper into an understanding of astrological influences, I became even more convinced of the power of intention and attraction.

As I mentioned earlier, I was also influenced by Ernest Holmes and Willis Kinnear's *Thoughts are Things*, which was published in 1967. As its title suggests, thoughts are things, and we attract what we think about. Our minds are gardens of thoughts and I believe we manifest and grow the seeds that we plant in our minds. So it was no surprise that I was attracted to Davidji's meditations, which take this one step further.

Attention—Intention with *Davidji*

Within about the first year of Tony's passing, I found a wonderful meditation group close to home. It was through this lovely group of ladies that I was introduced to a smart phone "app" called "Insight Timer."

This is a free app you can get on your phone through which you can select from 7,500 free meditations. Fortunately the ladies in the group had narrowed the field down for me, and I zeroed in on a meditation leader called *Davidji*. So now I make a concerted effort to keep a date with him in my living room every afternoon.

One of my favorite meditations is called "Attention—Intention." *Davidji* leads in by saying, ."Where attention goes, energy flows. What you place your attention on blossoms and blooms, and what you drift your attention away from withers, diminishes and dies.

"If we can truly learn that what we place our attention on elevates, and what we drift it from diminishes, then we would never grieve, we would never waste energy. We would never knowingly prolong pain.

"It all comes down to attention. Wherever it is, you are giving, consciously or unconsciously, power to that thing. Intention is a transformational property. Attention activates, intention transforms. When you are able to merge attention with intention, you can create the next unfolding."

So what is it that you would like to manifest into your life? Perhaps you're happy with your life just the way it is, or perhaps you are one of those ready for the next unfolding.

Manifesting my "bucket list"

A little more than two years after Tony passed, I was attending a local chamber of commerce social event when a friend of mine who is a travel agent was talking about a cruise—a trip to Barcelona that she was organizing. My ears immediately perked up. Barcelona was on my "bucket list."

My intention was to have a wonderful and memorable trip.

The cruise would actually depart from Barcelona and we arrived there two days prior to our planned departure. It so happened we arrived during Catalonia's demonstrations for independence, but fortunately they were all peaceful.

After touring Barcelona and enjoying its wonderful food and wine, we boarded our cruise ship. Our first port of call was Naples, Italy. We met our first tour guide and enjoyed a luxurious, comfortable bus ride to Pompeii, where we walked the streets with our guide.

Each day was a new port with a new tour guide as we enjoyed the breathtaking views of the mountainous Amalfi coast in the Salerno province in Southern Italy. To say that driving the Amalfi coast was breathtaking is putting it mildly.

We toured Positano, Sorrento, Vatican City and the ancient Coliseum. We shopped at the leather market in Florence, took pictures of Michelangelo's David and then went on to the Leaning Tower of Pisa, which was not at all what I expected. I was disappointed to find it very commercialized with a lot of vendors as you came through the entrance gates.

Then we went on to Cannes. Fortunately, it was not during the big film festival. Monaco was one of my favorite places. We got to see the changing of the guards and the church where Princess Grace and Prince Rainier were married. And of course, I was one of those who choose to hike up the mountain to see the famous Monte Carlo Casino. Our tour bus was not permitted in that area so we had to make the trek on foot. I was a little disappointed that I didn't get to gamble in the casino. There just wasn't enough time.

Our last port of call was Palma de Majorca, Spain, a place that I would love to return to and spend more time. This whole experience was a trip of a lifetime for me. The weather was perfect. The food and wine were magnificent and the friends and people that I was able to connect with during the trip were wonderful. The whole experience was everything and more than I could have intended it to be.

The trip of my second anniversary was much different than the meditative retreat that marked the first anniversary after Tony's passing. Had I spent the first anniversary on the cruise it would have left me empty. My needs were different then, as were my intentions and the energy that drew me to Hawaii for the Qigong introduction.

What have these two years taught me? As, Jon Kabat-Zinn, Author of *Full Catastrophe Living And Mindful Meditation In Everyday Life*, wrote:

"No matter where you go, there you are." You can run, you can travel the world, but you can't hide from yourself. You can stay busy working, volunteering, taking care of family, cooking and cleaning, watching TV or reading.

These are all among the things that make up a life, but they can be a way to hide from a life. It all depends on whether you are present in each moment. Wherever you go and whatever you are doing, there you are. Be there fully.

So I've come to the conclusion that the first and most important thing in life is to find peace and happiness within—essentially to be happy with yourself and allow yourself to believe it. That happier person you become will do well with connecting with others, and your better connected soul will be well fed. Learn to like yourself, and connecting will be second nature. Practice the art of connecting and feed your Soul!

Section Six

MORE THOUGHTS ON LONELINESS,
DEPRESSION AND HAPPINESS

*How do you know if you are suffering from
depression or loneliness?*
by Pragati Chauhan

Stop Trying to Be Happy
by Mark Manson

How Do You Know If You Are Suffering From Depression Or Loneliness?

How do you know if you are suffering from depression or simply feeling lonely? Having spoken with many people I know this is one of the big questions. It's one that I had often wondered about as I was going through the trials and tribulations of my own life. My questions were very clearly addressed in an article by author Pragati Chauhan which Dr. Sandra L. Brooks shared with me when I was doing my research. I have excerpted some of Ms. Pragati's answers and conclusions here.

Depression is not a feeling or a temporary emotion that makes you sulk about in your present situation, but is a mental disorder which makes you alienated both from yourself and the world. It shatters the bond that you share with your mind and soul. It happens in a way that the negative thoughts start controlling the way you look at the world and those around you.

Since depression is mood disorder it makes everything seem gloomy, threatening and impossible to you. Not every person who is depressed will have the same symptoms. But they do share one thing in common, that is isolating themselves from their loved ones. This happens mainly because they find themselves unworthy of being loved, of receiving care or venting out their emotions.

Well, reading Ms. Chauhan's words certainly made me feel better about myself because for the most part, I always want to be around people and doing something. In other words, I felt reassured that although I might feel lonely, I'm not clinically depressed.

The article continues ... "While loneliness can be a symptom of depression there is a huge difference between the two. In depression, people generally isolate themselves from others. They don't engage in activities they enjoyed doing earlier. They can't cherish the time spent with their loved ones as they feel numb."

Characteristics that define whether a person is suffering from depression or loneliness: Depression can be defined as an abnormal emotional state of mental disorder that affects how a person feels, thinks and behaves. It generally reflects on their behavioral patterns as they build walls around them that seem to be inescapable.

Loneliness is an absence of intimacy which leaves people with a void. Sadness, isolation and rejection are often linked with loneliness.

Clinical depression is a mental illness which disrupts your life and the way you perceive things. A depressed person can't find happiness in the things they cherished before. They are *always* surrounded by a pool of sadness that paints their life in blues.

However, loneliness is the feeling of emptiness either on being left alone or not finding a meaningful connection when surrounded by people.

Loneliness, on the other hand, can be cured by breaking social barriers, or engaging with warm company. A desired social connection and support can work well to revive lonely people.

Major Symptoms of Depression:

If you are not doing well lately and want to know whether it could be a warning or sign of depression look for these signs. To be diagnosed with depression a person needs to have at least five of the symptoms listed for a continued duration of at least two weeks or so.

- Having a depressed or irritable mood most of the time.
- Loss of interest in people, activity or things that give immense happiness before.
- A sudden change in weight, appetite, and behavior.
- Abnormal sleep patterns, disturbance in falling asleep or sleeping too much.
- Feeling tired, sluggish, stressed out and restless most of the times.
- Lack of confidence, low energy levels and sex drive.
- Finding your existence as unworthy, inappreciable and worthless in the society.
- Feeling hopeless, undesirable and guilty most of the times.
- Unable to concentrate or focus, loss of creativity and the ability to make petty decisions by yourself, during most days.
- Finding no meaning and purpose in life and the worst, having suicidal thoughts about ending your life.

Since the symptoms of depression may vary from person to person, it is advised to use this only as a guideline and before jumping to any conclusion do seek help from a mental health professional.

(Adapted from an article by Pragati Chauhan (www.getwellforever.com), which previously appeared in the Psychology Today and Huffington Post)

Stop Trying to Be Happy

Some people might name happiness as the opposite to depression. While it may be clear—if you are around a depressed person long enough—that they are not happy, that doesn't mean that simply overcoming depression or loneliness will result in happiness. What they do share is that the *Art of Connection* may lead away from one and toward the other.

Like loneliness and depression, happiness is often misunderstood as a concept. The following chapter borrows key points from an article by Mark Manson that examines what it means to be happy, and with that understanding, how one can make the journey to happiness.

If you have to try to be cool, Manson says, you will never be cool. If you have to try to be happy, then you will never be happy. Maybe the problem these days is people are just trying too hard.

Happiness, like other emotions, is not something you obtaim, but rather something you inhabit. When someone is angry, they are not thinking, "Am I finally angry? Am I doing this right?" No, you're out for blood. You inhabit and live the anger. You *are* the anger. And then it's gone.

Similarly, a confident man doesn't wonder if

he's confident, and a happy man does not wonder if he's happy. He simply is.

What this implies is that finding happiness is not something that is achieved in itself, but rather it is the side effect of a particular set of ongoing life experiences. This gets mixed up a lot, especially since happiness is marketed so much these days as a goal in and of itself. Buy X and be happy. Learn Y and be happy. But you can't buy happiness and you can't achieve happiness. It just is—once you get other parts of your life in order.

Happiness is Not the Same as Pleasure

When most people seek happiness, they are actually seeking pleasure: good food, more sex, more time for TV and movies, a new car, parties with friends, full body massages, losing 10 pounds, becoming more popular, and so on.

But while pleasure is great, it's not the same as happiness. Pleasure is correlated with happiness but does not cause it. Ask any drug addict how their pursuit of pleasure turned out. Ask an adulterer who shattered her family and lost her children whether pleasure ultimately made her happy. Ask a man who almost ate himself to death how happy pursuing pleasure made him feel.

Happiness is Not the Same as Positivity

It's a simple reality: unwelcome things do happen. Things go wrong. Mistakes are made and negative emotions arise. And that's fine. Negative emotions are necessary and healthy for maintaining a stable baseline happiness in one's life.

The trick with negative emotions is to 1) express them in a socially acceptable and healthy manner and 2) express them in a way which aligns with your values.

Happiness is the Process of Becoming Your Ideal Self

Completing a marathon makes us happier than eating a chocolate cake. Raising a child makes us happier than beating a video game. Starting a small business with friends and struggling to make money makes us happier than buying a new computer.

And the funny thing is that all three of the activities above are exceedingly *unpleasant* and require setting high expectations and potentially failing to always meet them. Yet, they are some of the most meaningful moments and activities of our lives. They involve pain, struggle, even anger and despair, yet once we've done them we look back and get misty-eyed about them.

Why? Because it's these sorts of activities that allow us to become our ideal selves. It's the perpetual pursuit of fulfilling our ideal selves that grants us happiness, regardless of superficial pleasures or pain, regardless of positive or negative emotions. This is why some people are happy in war and others are sad at weddings. It's why some are excited to work and others hate parties. The traits they're inhabiting don't align with their ideal selves.

The end results don't define our ideal selves. It's not finishing the marathon that makes us happy; it's achieving a difficult long-term goal that does.

And this is the reason that *trying* to be happy inevitably will make you unhappy. Because to try to be happy implies that you are not already inhabiting your ideal self, you are not aligned with the qualities of who you wish to be. After all, if you were acting out your ideal self, then you wouldn't feel the need to try to be happy.

Adapted from an article by Mark Manson (www.markmanson.net).

Made in the USA
Monee, IL
11 June 2025